LONGMAN LITERATURE

D0353784

Absurd Person Singular

Alan Ayckbourn

Editor: Geoff Barton

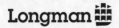

Contents

The writer on writing

by Alan Ayckbourn

The kingdom of the Hopcroft is at hand...

Absurd Person Singular was the fourth of my plays to be performed in London's West End although, like its predecessors, it started life in Scarborough in a modest 250-seat theatre-in-the-round. The auditorium was a makeshift affair; borrowed seats on rickety rostra in a small airless room of the public library. On the hot evenings, senior citizens would be supported from the theatre gasping for fresh sea air. Small children would, when carried away by the action, occasionally slip through the gaps in the seating and require rescuing. The stage floor was parquet and treacherously polished; the walls covered in untouchable, light green flock wallpaper. All in all an unpromising venue to present – as we saw it at the time – new work in new ways to new audiences.

For, despite the fact that the company – the brainchild initially of its founder, Stephen Joseph – had been running for fifteen years, theatre in the early seventies was still thought of largely as something done on a picture-frame stage, set apart from the audience. Heaven knows why. The proscenium arch was, as Stephen pointed out at the time, a comparatively recent invention in the overall scheme of things. Certainly the Greeks or the Elizabethans would have looked on it with some amazement.

Here we were, then, in the unlikeliest of towns in the most improbable of buildings presenting plays in an unusual setting with young unfamiliar casts to largely non-theatrical audiences. I can't pretend it wasn't a challenge. When we produced some particularly dark play – a verse drama about a young girl's journey to suicide was such a one, I seem to remember – on an especially bright seaside day, it was not uncommon to find ourselves performing to crowds of eight or nine.

The problem was that, on top of all the other disadvantages we were saddled with, our policy was wherever possible to present new work by new authors.

It was against this hand-to-mouth, improvised theatrical background that I was encouraged to write. First, during the late fifties and early sixties until his premature death in 1967, by Stephen Joseph himself; and then, as I gathered confidence, through my own volition.

By 1970, with seven or eight plays behind me – three of them international successes – I had taken over the Artistic Directorship of the Scarborough theatre. As a director, I was enjoying myself enormously, playing with this new toy I had somewhat fortuitously inherited. As a writer, though, I was anxious – whilst still working under the general heading of comedy – to explore fresh territory. I'd established through my earlier work (especially *Relatively Speaking* and *How the Other Half Loves*) that I could construct plays and that I could make audiences laugh. More important, they were coming back and what's more bringing their friends. Which meant that the tiny Library Theatre was now beginning to fill – not only for my plays but, as people got to hear about the company, for those of other, newer writers as well.

I wrote *Absurd Person Singular*, I remember, as I tend to write most of my plays, in a great hurry. It was due to be the second production of the 1972 Scarborough season. Before that, for two weeks in London we rehearsed, with me directing, a new version by David Campton of the classic vampire tale, *Carmilla*. During the evenings, throughout that fortnight, I wrote *Absurd Person Singular* for the rehearsing company of three men and three women. We opened *Carmilla* at the end of the fortnight for a one week pre-Scarborough 'tour' in the studio of the newly opened Sheffield Crucible Theatre.There we also started rehearsals for *Absurd* before moving on to Scarborough where, a week or so later, we finally opened the play to goodish, if not universally good, reviews.

I confess that it was, when it opened, half an hour too long. By the second night that had been remedied with some quite severe cutting. As it played in, too, it also gathered confidence and speed as the cast began to sense that they had a success. Audiences grew in size, and nightly response became increasingly enthusiastic.

Yet in rehearsal we had had our doubts – me most of all. The first act, at Sidney's and Jane's, seemed safe enough. I was pleased to have discovered the idea of 'offstage-action', to be sure. It seemed an interesting solution to set the scene apparently in the wrong room (the Hopcrofts' kitchen), in what was strictly speaking a 'backstage' area. Where we should have been, surely, was in the sitting-room. That's where the main action was happening – or so it seemed. Of course, it rarely was. The really interesting things, the things people want to say to each other in private were said in here by the sink. Besides, given that the other room contained Dick and Lottie Potter, it seemed an audience would only thank me for keeping us all out here, away from Dick's jokes.

None the less, although the act had one or two original constructional notions, it departed very little from the conventional lines of the comedy I had attempted earlier. Relating the play over three Christmases gave the play a sense of progression and, at the same time, a unity. I also liked the idea, following our glimpse of Jane's shiny, new-pin culinary unit in Act 1, of setting all the acts in various kitchens. It appealed to my sense of symmetry, besides supplying further dramatic unity. In addition, it was an ideal way to indicate the different social level that each of the three couples inhabited. Nowhere in the house says more about a person's habit and background, the nature of their day-to-day existence, than their kitchen. All well and good, so far.

It was in Act 2 that unknown, untried elements were introduced and fears began to arise. The idea of having the second act of a comedy centring on a woman trying to commit suicide (echoes of earlier verse dramas) seemed potentially very dangerous. Would we be accused of insensitivity and bad taste? Would the audience on the first night be filled with people trying to recover from their own unsuccessful suicide bids?

To counteract any charge that I was using human tragedy as a cheap way to get laughs – which was never my intention, of course – I resolved that, whatever happened, the humour would never be directed against the luckless Eva herself. The comedy would spring from a genuine, unmalicious misunderstanding; it would arise from the other misguided blunderers who had totally misread her intentions.

Indeed, as performances went by, I was to learn a vital comic lesson: namely that a single, truthful, serious event can become funny when set alongside a parallel series of equally serious, but contrasting events. The secret of the comedy in the second act (though I don't lay claim to having invented it!) is that all the characters – Eva, Sidney, Jane, Ronald, even the inebriated Marion – are behaving in a truthful, logical manner. All are unaware of the comedic possibilities of their plight. In order to appreciate it, they would need to be standing well back from it all; indeed, to be where we, the audience are.

More important, by taking their own situations entirely seriously, they present us with a choice of whether to laugh or sympathise: to recognise and relish or to identify and anguish. During the London run, Richard Briers, who played the ultimately crowing, vengeful Sidney with such demonic glee, told me that for every two visitors who came backstage to his dressing room, wet-eyed from seeing a performance, one blamed his or her condition on laughing, while the other blamed it on the shock of recognising either a close relative, or worse still, him or herself.

The second act became, despite our fears, the comic high point of the play.

In Act 3, I was again moving into fresh territory. The tone here is much more muted. A cold, bleak icebox of a kitchen. A dead central heating boiler and a dead marriage. Ronald, ironically, having lost any feelings he ever had, mournfully reads a soft porn novel with little sign of pleasure. Dick and Lottie have taken away for Christmas the sons he and Marion have never understood or bothered to communicate with much.

The underdogs are baying outside. Sidney and Jane are soon to arrive and demand that the others dance, literally, to the Hopcroft tune. Geoff and Eva have, meantime, fought each other to a standstill. Eva, now withdrawn, no longer presents anyone, most especially Geoff, with a vulnerable emotional target – or, conversely, with the smallest glimmer of warmth. Geoff, for his part, is emasculated by the failure of his work and the ultimate hollowness of his sexual infidelities.

Not perhaps the most promising of material upon which to build the last act of a comedy. Yet there is laughter, if of a more salutary kind. By now, we can no longer hide the fact entirely that we are not heading for the happiest of endings. Marion's emergence like a drunken spectre at a wake provides the final bleak-comic moment. All have been brought down by a weakness in their character. Marion through her vanity, Ronald his remoteness and indifference, Geoff his sexual and professional arrogance and Eva her self-centred self-obsession.

Only Sidney and Jane survive – but at what cost? Through an increasingly loveless, unfeeling, social-climbing partnership where the pursuit of material success is everything.

And the moral? Not that the Hopcrofts of this world will always rise and conquer. They needn't. But given the world we have where materialism does often seem to matter most, given what flawed emotional muddles most of us are anyway, the odds seem stacked heavily in favour of those with the least feelings or scruples and those with the strongest, most uncaring ambitions. I wheel and deal, therefore I am. Beware: the kingdom of the Hopcroft is at hand!

I mean, in this world it's dog eat dog, isn't it? No place for sentiment…when the chips are down it's every man for himself and blow you Jack, I regret to say.

Introduction

Writing a play

Alan Ayckbourn's approach to writing is not what you might traditionally expect of a playwright. His normal writing process is this: firstly, he works very quickly, setting aside a block of just four weeks to write a play. During this period he retreats from his full-time job as Artistic Director at the Stephen Joseph Theatre-in-the-Round in Scarborough. His play will have been scheduled into the theatre's season in advance, and the title possibly announced, even though he has not yet begun to write a single line.

With just four weeks earmarked for the writing of an entire play, you might expect Ayckbourn to spend every moment at his desk, writing frantically. But no: the deadline is still too far away. He says:

> I know that there's no way I'd start a play four weeks before it's due to go on. That just isn't the way I write. I know I've got to be within single figures of the opening date before there's any real chance.

> Ian Watson, *Conversations with Ayckbourn*

The first fortnight, then, of the writing period is spent killing time: watching television, sharpening pencils, going for walks, putting up shelves. No writing will take place. At the same time, though, Ayckbourn's mind will be at work on the new play, sifting ideas, perhaps returning to earlier plans, and rejecting most of what comes to the surface. All the while the date of the first rehearsal edges terrifyingly closer.

With possibly as few as ten days to go, Ayckbourn seems suddenly to recognise how short he is of time and the physical process of writing begins. He will start work late at night and write into the early hours of the morning, sometimes in longhand, sometimes dictating ideas directly to his personal assistant. Writing, he says, is on the whole *a lone and boring business* and you sense that it is a process which Ayckbourn must endure in order to reach the genuinely exciting part – the performance of his play:

At the moment, touch wood, ideas just pop out; as soon as I get one out, another one arrives, so that is nice, but there is always the fear that it won't happen, that there will be The Blank Sheet of Paper ... The best part of my work is not the clapping, it's the feeling at the end of the evening, that you have given the most wonderful party and those five hundred strangers who came in are feeling better.

Danny Danziger, *All in a Day's Work*

In Ayckbourn's normal pattern of writing, he clearly needs that self-imposed deadline, needs to feel the pressure building. This forces him to write. As we find so often, however, *Absurd Person Singular* differs slightly from the normal pattern, because Ayckbourn wrote the play at night whilst working full-time at the theatre during the day directing the first play of the season. (He refers to this in 'The writer on writing' at the beginning of this edition, page vi.) His own play, as yet unwritten of course, was the next scheduled production:

I remember going into a rehearsal of Carmilla and saying, 'Anybody know any forfeits?' And somebody said 'Orange between the knees.' And I said, 'Oh, thanks very much!' People in the cast wondered what was going on! That's how that was done.

Conversations with Ayckbourn

These are the circumstances, then, in which the play was written: the looming deadline, the full day's work in the theatre which could furnish the author with some additional bits of stage business, whilst the writing itself was taking place through the night.

A dark comedy

That was a strange play, Alan Ayckbourn has said of *Absurd Person Singular*. You only have to consider the title to see how strange it is. As we have seen, Ayckbourn sometimes thinks up his titles before he starts to write his plays. They tend to be well-known phrases, or clichés, such as *Standing Room Only*, *Joking Apart*, *Ten Times Table*, and *Season's Greetings*. But *Absurd Person Singular* is different: it does not, on its own, seem to make much sense.

The first point to note is that the title has very little to do with the play itself. It was originally the title of a totally different play. Once Alan Ayckbourn had abandoned that and begun to write this play, he decided to use this title – because he liked it. It is worth recognising this fact in advance, because some people have spent a good deal of time concocting ingenious theories as to what the title might mean and how it might relate to the events of the play. *Absurd Person Singular* is a play on words (Ayckbourn is fond of these). In talking about the structure of language, we can refer to the first person singular (*I*, *me*) or to the third person singular (*she*, *he*, *her* and so on). Ayckbourn has simply switched in that unexpected word *absurd* to create a quirky and memorable title.

The play is strange for other reasons. It is a comedy, and at times it splits apart into ridiculous, uncontrollable farce, as characters misunderstand each other, ignore each other, or try – disastrously – to help each other. In Act 2, for example, Eva's attempts at suicide cause a chain of hilarious mishaps. But perhaps you can already sense something strange: the words *comedy*, *farce* and *hilarious* are rubbing uneasily against that very different, darker word *suicide*. What kind of subject is that for a comic play?

Alan Ayckbourn has said that with *Absurd Person Singular*, which he wrote in 1972, he began to explore dark comedy, a form of comic writing which makes us laugh but, at the same time, causes us to feel uncomfortable:

> *I discovered that I could start to strip the layers off the people a little bit and find, perhaps, less typical emotions than you can find in your average light comedy, like anger and jealousy and fear and rage and lust: I mean real, burning, destructive desire …*
>
> *Conversations with Ayckbourn*

With words like these around, the term *comedy* itself begins to strain. The effect of watching characters who make us laugh, but whose obsessions and failings are increasingly visible, can make for uncomfortable entertainment. Producers of the play have observed that Act 2 generates the most laughter in an audience, whilst Act 3, which you would traditionally expect to be the comic highpoint, tends to have a more subdued comic effect. This is no accident: when the American producers asked to switch around the second and third acts because they wanted the performance to *end on a high*, Ayckbourn refused.

Similarly, in his own most recent production, in Scarborough and London in 1990, the party games which end the play were abruptly halted by unnerving chords and a sinister, single spotlight in the darkness. The final image was of Sidney Hopcroft silhouetted as the small, barking tyrant determined to get his own way. The chill ending to the play is clearly designed to disturb.

Characters

Absurd Person Singular might seem a rather remote play to some readers at first sight. Here we have three distinct acts in one play, each set in a kitchen, each with the same cast of six characters, each taking place at a Christmas party. The characters are middle-aged, middle-class, and married.

In middle age many people become obsessed with reviewing their lives, wondering whether they have been successful in their careers and in their relationships. *Absurd Person Singular* questions what it means to be considered a success. In Act 1 Sidney and Jane Hopcroft are eager to impress their guests with a successful party. With guests of some importance coming around – a bank manager, an architect – Sidney has the opportunity to make a strong impression on people who in the future *can be very, very useful to us…* (page 34). Success, in these terms, is associated with career – *men's* careers. Jane's role is to be the efficient wife, someone who will reflect well upon her husband and not cause him embarrassment. Obsessed with naval precision, Sidney has given Jane specific responsibilities: *…buying the beverages*, he reminds her, *was your department* (page 18).

We might sneer at this patronising attitude, but Jane clearly feels a terrifying weight of responsibility: *I want it to be right … I don't want you to be let down. Not by me. I want it to look good for you. I don't want to let you down…*(page 5).

Jane's words are charged with growing panic that she might fail to live up to Sidney's standards. His reply – typically – serves only to wind her fears tighter: *You never have yet…*, he tells her (page 5). That word *yet* is loaded with the suggestion that, in Sidney's eyes, Jane cannot fully be trusted to make a success of her role. Sure enough, one oversight on her part –

forgetting to stock up with tonic water – and Sidney piles on the moral pressure: *I hope you haven't let us down*, he says snidely (page 18).

The play warns us that traditional career success can be unpredictable. Small-time businessman Sidney Hopcroft is a figure of fun in the first two acts, distanced from conversation and jokes which he does not really understand. His language marks him out from the others: it is tangled with clichés, as here when he discusses business with Ronald:

SIDNEY   I mean, in this world it's dog eat dog, isn't it? No place for sentiment. Not in business. I mean, all right, so on occasions you can scratch mine. I'll scratch yours ...

RONALD   Beg your pardon?

SIDNEY   Tit for tat. But when the chips are down it's every man for himself and blow you Jack, I regret to say ...

Act 1, page 27

Sidney's stale use of English is a mark of his character and of his class. It is often said that the English are obsessed with class and *Absurd Person Singular* provides evidence of this. Marion looks contemptuously down upon the Hopcrofts' *loathsome little house* (page 32); Geoffrey points out that such homes are designed for people who are not well off and who *aren't particularly choosey* (page 33). Where you live – and the décor of your kitchen – reveals not only who you are, but also your level of social success.

By Act 3, though, Sidney's career has overtaken the established professions of banker and architect and we see Ronald and Geoffrey both uneasily dependent on his money and favour. The play, from back in the early seventies, already foresaw the growing association between money and success.

Where do the female characters fit into this scheme of success? Here again the play disturbs. Jane, we quickly recognise, finds social situations stressful and awkward. Still dripping from an evening largely spent in the rain, rather than attending her own party, she retreats at the end of the first act to the security of the kitchen sink:

As she cleans she seems to relax. Softly at first, then louder, she is heard to sing happily to herself ...

Act 1, page 35

Her confidence frequently undermined by her husband, Jane is able to feel success only in a role which is entirely her own. Whilst Sidney disappears to watch television, delighted with the success of his party, Jane escapes into her isolated area of expertise: cleaning up.

Marion's life, meanwhile, has lost its purpose and she too seeks a retreat — into drink; whilst Eva, in Act 2, aims at a last desperate form of escape, with her various inept attempts at suicide. Shockingly, and hilariously, no one really notices.

This is perhaps the central point of the play — that however good-spirited the characters may seem on occasions, as in their individual attempts to assist Eva, they are all trapped in their own small, shuttered worlds. As Ayckbourn has said:

> I'm really showing how sad it is that people can try to be nice and that it sometimes doesn't work. I'm saying that a lot of the worst things that happen in life are the result of well-meaning actions.

Interview in In Britain

The characters respond to a woman's emotional crisis by cleaning the oven, unblocking the sink or mending a light, a retreat into trivia. No one truly communicates with anyone or understands anyone. Geoff lectures Eva about their marriage but he is clearly talking to himself, thinly reassuring himself that his selfishness in abandoning Eva is in the interests of both of them. Ronald, later, openly confesses his failure to understand his wife:

> I mean, this may sound ridiculous, but I've never to this day really known what most women think about anything. Completely closed book to me. I mean, God bless them, what would we do without them? But I've never understood them.

Act 3, page 75

As a consequence he sinks further into his own drifting existence, locked in a (literally) icy marriage, and blind to his wife Marion's increasing dependency on drink.

By Act 3 Eva has taken over responsibility not only for her own but also for her husband's life, but we sense that it is only a brief lull in open hostilities. No affection remains. The play shows us not only the stagnating nature of marriage, but also the failure of human beings to understand one another.

From Marion's inability to fathom the Hopcrofts' explanation of their washing machine to the failure of all the characters to recognise Eva's attempts at suicide, *Absurd Person Singular* shows us how hollow human relationships can be underneath the frail surface of politeness.

Structure

Absurd Person Singular at first appears quite traditional in its structure, with its three acts, set in three kitchens, over a period of three years. The format is satisfyingly symmetrical: in each act the rhythm of the action is the same, always beginning in a low-key fashion with two characters on stage in conversation. Then as the other characters arrive the tempo quickens, characters' words and actions collide, and events become increasingly frantic. Beneath the top layers of high comedy, you find the solid structure of a well-made play, evidence of Ayckbourn's theatrical craftsmanship.

However true it might be to describe the structure in these neat terms, you quickly realise as you read or watch the play that this is no conventional comedy. Most theatre-goers would probably expect a play which was set at three suburban parties to take place in three suburban sitting-rooms; they would expect to see the guests chatting, laughing, eating and drinking. When Ayckbourn began to write the play it was essentially like this, as he says in 'The writer on writing' on page vii. *The really interesting things*, he then realised, were *said in here by the sink*, and he shifted the action of the play to the kitchen.

One of the most obvious effects of this rewriting is that the two characters who dominate the first two Christmas parties with their conversation, laughter and generally boisterous behaviour are never actually seen on stage because they do not (thankfully) come into the kitchen. From time to time we hear Dick and Lottie Potter's voices drifting in from the sitting-room before the kitchen door closes; in Act 2 we hear Dick manically entertaining the Jacksons' dog, George. As an audience, however, *we have the good fortune never to meet* the Potters in person, as Ayckbourn notes with some relief in his stage directions on page 6. These two hearty schoolteachers are doomed to live for ever off-stage.

This is one of a number of running jokes in the play, theatrical effects which remind us that Ayckbourn's techniques grew out of his background as, initially, a stage manager and, later, a director. As you read the play you notice how various characters refer to seemingly trivial events – Marion's drinking, George's barking, Jane's tendency to spill food and drink in company – and you see how they become increasingly important in the chain of events.

This technique reminds us how well constructed the play is, tying together the events of the various acts and preparing us for the twists to come. There is a danger also that ingenious plotting of this kind hijacks the play. As you read Act 2, try to pinpoint the moment at which the play shifts from social comedy, in which we laugh at the way characters talk and behave, to farce. In farce, events spin round, dragging characters with them, and become important for their own sake, rather than for the light they shed on the characters: plots become increasingly improbable. See how you respond to this. Do the frenzied misunderstandings of the second act build up convincingly? Or does the play sacrifice some of its seriousness as it shifts into ever higher comic gear?

These questions might irritate you and perhaps you will reply: *But why shouldn't the play simply entertain us? Why must there be a serious point?* Alternatively, you might find that the laughter actually increases the sadness of Eva's suicide attempt; the more you laugh, perhaps the more disturbing the subject-matter seems.

Whichever of these is your response, notice the sheer nerve with which Alan Ayckbourn writes, structuring his play in such a way that its comic high-spot is built around a woman's efforts to kill herself. In another writer's hands the act could have become distasteful. Here it verges on farce of a dangerous kind. Whether you agree or not that the risk pays off, you have to admire the boldness of the idea.

Preparing to read

This might seem an unnecessary topic to include here, but if you want to gain the greatest pleasure from *Absurd Person Singular*, it is important to plan your reading of it. There is, after all, something artificial about reading a play.

It was written to be performed. Whilst actors, obviously, would start by reading aloud from the script, they would quite quickly move on to rehearsing without copies of the text, perhaps only then starting to breathe life into the lines and characters. You need to aim to do this *whilst reading*, so that the life is not ground out of the play or the humour flattened.

Whether you are reading in small groups or in one larger group, you need to assign a number of parts: besides the six characters mentioned in the cast list, you will also need two people to play Dick and Lottie Potter, one person to play George the dog, and someone to read the main stage directions.

With parts assigned, it would be ideal if those reading could spend some time looking through the play, getting the feel of their characters' personalities and beginning to work on a style of delivering the lines. It is important that those reading feel confident with their characters, so that the humour of the play builds up naturally.

It would probably be best to read one act per lesson (Act 1 and Act 2 each take between forty-five and fifty-five minutes to read aloud; Act 3 requires rather less than this), leaving time for discussion at the end. Remember also that there is a glossary on page 93 at the end of the play, with questions after each act to help you to focus your thoughts. These notes are designed to reduce the need to keep interrupting the play simply to explain expressions that are not familiar. Keep the pace of the play moving and you will enjoy the humour all the more.

Reading log

One of the easiest ways of keeping track of your reading is to keep a log book. This can be any exercise book or folder that you have to hand, but make sure you reserve it exclusively for reflecting on your reading, both at home and in school.

As you read the play, stop from time to time and think back over what you have read.

- Is there anything that puzzles you? Note down some questions that you might want to research, discuss with your friends, or ask a teacher. Also note any quotations which strike you as important or memorable.

- Does your reading remind you of anything else you have read, heard or seen on TV or the cinema? Jot down what it is and where the similiarities lie.

- Have you had any experiences similiar to those narrated in the play? Do you find yourself identifying closely with one or more of the characters? Record this as accurately as you can.

- Do you find yourself really liking, or really loathing, any of the characters? What is it about them that makes you feel so strongly? Make notes that you can add to.

- Can you picture the locations and settings? Draw maps, plans, diagrams, drawings, in fact any doodle that helps you make sense of these things.

- Now and again try to predict what will happen next in the play. Use what you already know of the author, the genre (type of story) and the characters to help you do this. Later record how close you were and whether you were surprised at the outcome.

- Write down any feelings that you have about the play. Your reading log should help you to make sense of your own ideas alongside those of the author.

Absurd Person Singular

Absurd Person Singular

First produced at the Library Theatre, Scarborough, in June
1972 and subsequently by Michael Codron at the Criterion
Theatre, London, on 4 July 1973, with the following cast:

SIDNEY	Richard Briers
JANE	Bridget Turner
RONALD	Michael Aldridge
MARION	Sheila Hancock
GEOFFREY	David Burke
EVA	Anna Calder-Marshall

The play directed by Eric Thompson
Settings by Alan Tagg
ACT I   Sidney and Jane's Kitchen. Last Christmas
ACT II   Geoffrey and Eva's Kitchen. This Christmas
ACT III   Ronald and Marion's Kitchen. Next Christmas

Time – the present

Act One

Sidney and Jane Hopcroft's kitchen of their small suburban house. Last Christmas

Although on a modest scale, it is a model kitchen. Whilst not containing all the gadgetry, it does have an automatic washing machine, a fridge, an electric cooker and a gleaming sink unit. All these are contained or surrounded by smart formica-topped working surfaces with the usual drawers and cupboards. The room also contains a small table, also formica-topped, and matching chairs

When the CURTAIN rises, Jane, a woman in her thirties, is discovered bustling round wiping the floor, cupboard doors, working surfaces – in fact, anything in sight – with a cloth. She sings happily as she works. She wears a pinafore and bedroom slippers, but, under this, a smart new party dress. She is unimaginatively made up and her hair is tightly permed. She wears rubber gloves to protect her hands

As Jane works, Sidney enters, a small dapper man of about the same age. He has a small trimmed moustache and a cheery, unflappable manner. He wears his best, rather old-fashioned, sober suit. A dark tie, polished hair and shoes complete the picture

SIDNEY   Hallo, hallo. What are we up to out here, eh?
JANE   (*without pausing in her work*) Just giving it a wipe.
SIDNEY   Dear oh dear. Good gracious me. Does it need it? Like a battleship. Just like a battleship. They need you in the Royal Navy.
JANE   (*giggling*) Silly . . .
SIDNEY   No – the Royal Navy.
JANE   Silly . . .

Sidney goes to the back door, turns the Yale knob, opens it and sticks his hand out

SIDNEY   Still raining, I see.

1

JANE   Shut the door, it's coming in.

SIDNEY   Cats and dogs. Dogs and cats. (*He shuts the door, wiping his wet hand on his handkerchief. Striding to the centre of the room and staring up at his digital clock, in the 'fourth wall'*) Eighteen-twenty-three. (*Consulting his watch*) Eighteen-twenty-three. Getting on. Seven minutes → they'll be here.

JANE   Oh. (*She straightens up and looks round the kitchen for somewhere she's missed*)

SIDNEY   I've got a few games lined up.

JANE   Games?

SIDNEY   Just in case.

JANE   Oh good.

SIDNEY   I've made a parcel for 'Pass the Parcel', sorted out a bit of music for musical bumps and thought out a few forfeits.

JANE   Good.

SIDNEY   I've thought up some real devils. (*He puts his leg on the table*)

JANE   I bet. (*She knocks his leg off, and wipes*)

SIDNEY   Just in case. Just in case things need jollying up. (*Seeing Jane still wiping*) I don't want to disappoint you but we're not going to be out here for our drinks, you know.

JANE   Yes, I know.

SIDNEY   The way you're going . . .

JANE   They might want to look . . .

SIDNEY   I doubt it.

JANE   The ladies might.

SIDNEY   (*chuckling knowingly*) I don't imagine the wife of a banker will particularly choose to spend her evening in our kitchen. Smart as it is.

JANE   No?

SIDNEY   I doubt if she spends very much time in her own kitchen. Let alone ours.

JANE   Still . . .

SIDNEY   Very much the lady of leisure, Mrs Brewster-Wright. Or so I would imagine.

JANE   What about Mrs Jackson?

SIDNEY   (*doubtfully*) Well – again, not a woman you think of in the same breath as you would a kitchen.

JANE   All women are interested in kitchens. (*She turns to the sink*)

SIDNEY   (*ironically*) Oh, if you're looking for a little job . . .

JANE   What's that?

SIDNEY   A small spillage. My fault.

JANE   (*very alarmed*) Where?

SIDNEY   In there. On the sideboard.

JANE   Oh, Sidney. (*She snatches up an assortment of cloths, wet and dry*)

SIDNEY   Nothing serious.

JANE   Honestly.

Sidney goes to the back door, opens it, sticks a hand out

SIDNEY   Dear oh dear. (*He closes the door and dries his hand on his handkerchief*)

JANE   (*returning*) Honestly.

SIDNEY   Could you see it?

JANE   You spoil that surface if you leave it. You leave a ring. (*She returns her dish cloth to the sink, her dry cloths to the drawer and now takes out a duster and a tin of polish*) Now that room's going to smell of polish. I had the windows open all day so it wouldn't.

SIDNEY   Well then, don't polish.

JANE   I have to polish. There's a mark. (*She goes to the door and then pauses*) I know, bring the air freshener.

SIDNEY   Air freshener?

JANE   Under the sink.

Jane exits

SIDNEY   Ay, ay, Admiral. (*He whistles a sailor's horn-pipe, amused*) Dear oh dear. (*He opens the cupboard under the sink, rummages and brings out an aerosol tin. He is one of those men who like to read all small print. This he does, holding the tin at arm's*

3

length to do so. *Reading*) 'Shake can before use.' (*He does so. Reading*) 'Remove cap.' (*He does so. Reading*) 'Hold away from body and spray into air by depressing button.' (*He holds the can away from his body, points it in the air and depresses the button. The spray hisses out over his shirt front*) Dear oh dear. (*He puts down the tin, wipes his shirt-front with a dishcloth*)

Jane enters

JANE What are you doing?

SIDNEY Just getting this to rights. Just coming to terms with your air freshener.

JANE That's the fly spray.

SIDNEY Ah.

JANE Honestly. (*She takes the canister from him and puts it on top of the washing machine*)

SIDNEY My mistake.

JANE For someone who's good at some things you're hopeless.

SIDNEY Beg your pardon, Admiral, beg your pardon.

Jane puts away the duster and polish

(*Checking his watch with the clock*) Four and a half minutes to go.

JANE And you've been at those nuts, haven't you?

SIDNEY Nuts?

JANE In there. In the bowl. On the table. Those nuts. You know the ones I mean.

SIDNEY I may have had a little dip. Anyway, how did you know I'd been at those nuts? Eh? How did you know, old eagle-eye?

JANE Because I know how I left them. Now come on, out of my way. Don't start that. I've got things to do.

SIDNEY (*closing with her*) What about a kiss then?

JANE (*trying to struggle free*) Sidney . . .

SIDNEY Come on. Christmas kiss.

JANE Sidney. No, not now. What's the matter with you? Sidney . . . (*She pauses, sniffing*)

4

SIDNEY   What's the matter now?

JANE   What's that smell?

SIDNEY   Eh?

JANE   It's on your tie. What's this smell on your tie?

They both sniff his tie

There. Can you smell?

SIDNEY   Oh, that'll be the fly spray.

JANE   Fly spray?

SIDNEY   Had a bit of a backfire.

JANE   It's killed off your after-shave.

SIDNEY   (*jovially*) As long as it hasn't killed off my flies, eh.
(*He laughs*)

Jane laughs

(*Suddenly cutting through this*) Eighteen-twenty-eight. Two
minutes.

JANE   (*nervous again*) I hope everything's all right.

SIDNEY   When?

JANE   For them. I want it to be right.

SIDNEY   Of course it's right.

JANE   I mean. I don't want you to be let down. Not by me.
I want it to look good for you. I don't want to let you
down . . .

SIDNEY   You never have yet . . .

JANE   No, but it's special tonight, isn't it? I mean, with Mr
and Mrs Brewster-Wright and Mr and Mrs Jackson. It's
important.

SIDNEY   Don't forget Dick and Lottie Potter. They're coming,
too.

JANE   Oh, well, I don't count Dick and Lottie. They're
friends.

SIDNEY   I trust by the end of this evening, we shall all be
friends. Just don't get nervous. That's all. Don't get nervous.
(*He consults the clock and checks it with his watch*) One minute
to go.

5

A slight pause. The front door chimes sound

What was that?

JANE   The front door.

SIDNEY   They're early. Lucky we're ready for them.

JANE   Yes. (*In a sudden panic*) I haven't sprayed the room.

SIDNEY   All right, all right. You can do it whilst I'm letting them in. Plenty of time.

JANE   It doesn't take a second.

Jane snatches up the air freshener and follows Sidney out into the sitting-room. A silence. Jane comes hurrying back into the kitchen

Jane puts away the air freshener, removes her pinny, straightens her clothing and hair in the mirror, creeps back to the kitchen door and opens it a chink. Voices are heard – Sidney's and two others. One is a jolly hearty male voice and one a jolly hearty female voice. They are Dick and Lottie Potter, whom we have the good fortune never to meet in person, but quite frequently hear whenever the door to the kitchen is open. Both have loud, braying, distinctive laughs. Jane closes the door, cutting off the voices, straightens her hair and dress for the last time, looking at a mirror in the 'fourth wall', grips the door handle, takes a deep breath, is about to make her entrance into the room when she sees she is still wearing her bedroom slippers

Oh.

She takes off her slippers, puts them on the table and scuttles round the kitchen looking for her shoes. She cannot find them. She picks up the slippers and wipes the table with their fluffy side, where they have made a mark

Oh.

She hurries back to the door, opens it a fraction. Jolly chatter and laughter is heard. Jane stands for a long time, peeping through the crack in the door, trying to catch sight of her shoes. She sees them. She closes the door again. She stands lost

Oh. Oh. Oh.

The door opens. Loud laughter from off. Sidney comes in laughing.
He closes the door. The laughter cuts off abruptly

SIDNEY *(fiercely, in a low voice)* Come on. What are you doing?

JANE I can't.

SIDNEY What?

JANE I've got no shoes.

SIDNEY What do you mean, no shoes?

JANE They're in there.

SIDNEY Where?

JANE By the fireplace. I left them so I could slip them on.

SIDNEY Well, then, why didn't you?

JANE I didn't have time. I forgot.

SIDNEY Well, come and get them.

JANE No . . .

SIDNEY It's only Dick and Lottie Potter.

JANE You fetch them.

SIDNEY I can't fetch them.

JANE Yes, you can. Pick them up and bring them in here.

SIDNEY But I . . .

JANE Sidney, please.

SIDNEY Dear oh dear. What a start. I say, what a start. *(He opens the door cautiously and listens. Silence)* They've stopped talking.

JANE Have they?

SIDNEY Wondering where we are, no doubt.

JANE Well, go in. Here.

SIDNEY What?

JANE *(handing him her slippers)* Take these.

SIDNEY What do I do with these?

JANE The hall cupboard.

SIDNEY You're really expecting rather a lot tonight, aren't you?

JANE I'm sorry.

SIDNEY Yes, well it's got to stop. It's got to stop. I have to entertain out there, you know. *(He opens the door and starts laughing heartily as he does so)*

7

Sidney goes out, closing the door

Jane hurries about nervously, making still more adjustments to her person and checking her appearance in the mirror

At length the door opens, letting in a bellow of laughter. Sidney returns, carrying Jane's shoes

(*Behind him*) Yes, I will. I will. I'll tell her that, Dick ... (*He laughs until he's shut the door. His laugh cuts off abruptly. Thrusting Jane's shoes at her, ungraciously*) Here.

JANE   Oh, thank goodness.

SIDNEY   Now for heaven's sake, come in.

JANE   (*struggling into her shoes*) Yes, I'm sorry. What did Dick say?

SIDNEY   When?

JANE   Just now? That you told him you'd tell me.

SIDNEY   I really can't remember. Now then, are you ready?

JANE   Yes, yes.

SIDNEY   It's a good job it's only Dick and Lottie out there. It might have been the Brewster-Wrights. I'd have had a job explaining this to them. Walking in and out like a shoe salesman. All right?

JANE   Yes.

SIDNEY   Right. (*He throws open the door, jovially*) Here she is. (*Pushing Jane ahead of him*) Here she is at last.

Hearty cries of 'Ah ha' from Dick and Lottie

JANE   (*going in*) Here I am.

Jane and Sidney exit

SIDNEY   (*closing the door behind him*) At last.

A silence. A long one.

Sidney returns to the kitchen. Conversation is heard as he opens and closes the door. He starts hunting round the kitchen opening drawers and not bothering to shut them. After a second, the door opens again, and Jane comes in

JANE   (*as she enters*) Yes, well you say that to Lottie, not to me. I don't want to know that . . . (*She closes the door*) What are you doing? Oh, Sidney, what are you doing? (*She hurries round after him, closing the drawers*)

SIDNEY   Bottle-opener. I'm trying to find the bottle-opener. I can't get the top off Lottie's bitter lemon.

JANE   It's in there.

SIDNEY   In there?

JANE   Why didn't you ask me?

SIDNEY   Where in there?

JANE   On the mantelpiece.

SIDNEY   The mantelpiece?

JANE   It looks nice on the mantelpiece.

SIDNEY   It's no use having a bottle-opener on a mantelpiece, is it? I mean, how am I . . . ?

The door chimes sound

JANE   Somebody else.

SIDNEY   All right, I'll go. I'll go. You open the bitter lemon. With gin.

JANE   Gin and bitter lemon.

SIDNEY   And shake the bottle first.

Sidney opens the door. Silence from the room. He goes out, closing it

JANE   (*to herself*) Gin and bitter lemon – shake the bottle first – gin and bitter lemon – shake the bottle first . . . (*She returns to the door and opens it very slightly. There can now be heard the chatter of five voices. She closes the door and feverishly straightens herself*)

The door opens a crack and Sidney's nose appears. Voices are heard behind him

SIDNEY   (*hissing*) It's them.

JANE   Mr and Mrs Brewster-Wright?

SIDNEY   Yes. Ronald and Marion. Come in.

JANE Ronald and Marion.

SIDNEY Come in.

Sidney opens the door wider, grabs her arm, jerks her through the door and closes it

JANE *(as she is dragged in)* Gin and bitter lemon – shake the bottle first . . .

Silence. Another fairly long one. The door bursts open and Jane comes rushing out

Murmur of voices

(Over her shoulder) Wait there! Just wait there! *(She dashes to the sink and finds a tea towel and two dish cloths)*

Ronald, a man in his mid-forties, enters. Impressive, without being distinguished. He is followed by an anxious Sidney. Ronald, holding one leg of his trousers away from his body. He has evidently got drenched

SIDNEY Oh dear oh dear. I'm terribly sorry.

RONALD That's all right. Can't be helped.

JANE Here's a cloth.

RONALD Oh, thank you – yes, yes. *(He takes the tea towel)* I'll just use this one, if you don't mind.

SIDNEY Well, what a start, eh? What a grand start to the evening. *(With a laugh)* Really, Jane.

JANE I'm terribly sorry. I didn't realize it was going to splash like that.

RONALD Well, tricky things, soda siphons. You either get a splash or a dry gurgle. Never a happy medium.

JANE Your nice suit.

RONALD Good God, it's only soda water. Probably do it good, eh?

JANE I don't know about that.

RONALD *(returning the tea towel)* Thanks very much. Well, it's wet enough outside there. I didn't expect to get wet inside as well.

10

SIDNEY   No, no . . .

JANE   Terribly sorry.

RONALD   Accidents happen. Soon dry out. I'll run around for a bit.

SIDNEY   I'll tell you what. I could let you have a pair of my trousers from upstairs just while yours dry.

JANE   Oh, yes.

RONALD   No, no. That's all right. I'll stick with these. Hate to break up the suit, eh? (*He laughs*)

So do Sidney and Jane

Marion, a well-groomed woman, a little younger than Ronald and decidedly better preserved, comes in

MARION   All right, darling?

RONALD   Yes, yes.

MARION   Oh! (*She stops short in the doorway*) Isn't this gorgeous? Isn't this enchanting?

JANE   Oh.

MARION   What a simply dishy kitchen. (*To Jane*) Aren't you lucky?

JANE   Well . . .

MARION   It's so beautifully arranged. Ronnie, don't you agree? Isn't this splendid?

RONALD   Ah.

MARION   Just look at these working surfaces and you must have a gorgeous view from that window, I imagine.

SIDNEY   Well . . .

MARION   It must be stunning. You must look right over the fields at the back.

SIDNEY   No – no.

JANE   No, we just look into next door's fence.

MARION   Well, which way are the fields?

JANE   I've no idea.

MARION   How extraordinary. I must be thinking of somewhere else.

SIDNEY   Mind you, we've got a good ten yards to the fence . . .

11

RONALD   On a clear day, eh?

SIDNEY   Beg pardon?

MARION   Oh look, Ronnie, do come and look at these cupboards.

RONALD   Eh?

MARION   Look at these, Ronnie. (*Opening and shutting the cupboard doors*) They're so easy to open and shut.

JANE   Drawers – here, you see . . .

MARION   Drawers! (*Opening them*) Oh, lovely deep drawers. Put all sorts of things in these, can't you? And then just shut it up and forget them.

SIDNEY   Yes, yes, they're handy for that . . .

MARION   No, it's these cupboards. I'm afraid I really do envy you these. Don't you envy them, Ronnie?

RONALD   I thought we had cupboards.

MARION   Yes, darling, but they're nothing like these. Just open and shut that door. It's heaven.

RONALD   (*picking up a booklet from the counter*) Cupboard's a cupboard. (*He sits and reads*)

JANE   (*proudly*) Look. (*Going to the washing machine*) Sidney's Christmas present to me . . .

MARION   (*picking up the air freshener from the top of the washing machine*) Oh lovely. What is it? Hair spray?

SIDNEY   No, no. That's the fly spray, no. My wife meant the machine. (*He takes the spray from her and puts it down*)

MARION   Machine?

JANE   Washing machine. Here . . .

MARION   Oh, that's a washing machine. Tucked under there. How thrilling. What a marvellous Christmas present.

JANE   Well, yes.

MARION   Do tell me, how did you manage to keep it a surprise from her?

SIDNEY   Well . . .

MARION   I mean, don't tell me he hid it or wrapped it up. I don't believe it.

SIDNEY   No, I just arranged for the men to deliver it and plumb it in.

JANE   They flooded the kitchen.

MARION   Super.

JANE   You see, it's the automatic. It's got – all the programmes and then spin-drying and soak.

MARION   Oh, good heavens. Ronnie, come here at once and see this.

RONALD   (*reading avidly*) Just coming . . .

MARION   (*bending to read the dial*) What's this? Whites – coloureds – my God, it's apartheid.

JANE   Beg pardon?

MARION   What's this? Minimum icon? What on earth is that?

JANE   No, minimum iron.

MARION   Don't tell me it does the ironing too.

JANE   Oh, no, it . . .

MARION   Ronnie, have you seen this extraordinary machine?

RONALD   Yes. Yes . . .

MARION   It not only does your washing and your whites and your blacks and your coloureds and so on, it does your ironing.

SIDNEY   No, no . . .

JANE   No . . .

MARION   (*to Jane*) We shall soon be totally redundant. (*She picks up the spray and fires it into the air and inhales*) What a poignant smell. It's almost too good to waste on flies, isn't it. Now where . . . ? It's a little like your husband's gorgeous cologne, surely?

JANE   Oh, well . . .

The doorbell chimes

MARION   Oh, good gracious. What was that? Does that mean your shirts are cooked or something?

SIDNEY   No, front doorbell.

MARION   Oh, I see. How pretty.

SIDNEY   Somebody else arrived.

JANE   Yes, I'd better . . .

SIDNEY   Won't be a minute.

JANE   No, I'll go.
SIDNEY   No . . .
JANE   No, I'll go.

Jane hurries out, closing the door

MARION   I do hope your Mr and Mrs Potter don't feel terribly abandoned in there. They're splendidly jolly, blooming people, aren't they?
SIDNEY   Yes, Dick's a bit of a laugh.
MARION   Enormous. Now, you must tell me one thing, Mr Hopcroft. How on earth did you squeeze that machine so perfectly under the shelf? Did you try them for size or were you terribly lucky?
SIDNEY   No, I went out and measured the machine in the shop.
MARION   Oh, I see.
SIDNEY   And then I made the shelf, you see. So it was the right height.
MARION   No, I mean how on earth did you know it was going to be right?
SIDNEY   Well, that's the way I built it.
MARION   No. You don't mean this is you?
SIDNEY   Yes, yes. Well, the shelf is.
MARION   Ronnie!
RONALD   Um?
MARION   Ronnie, darling, what are you reading?
RONALD   (*vaguely consulting the cover of his book*) Er . . .
SIDNEY   Ah, that'll be the instruction book for the stove.
RONALD   Oh, is that what it is? I was just trying to work out what I was reading. Couldn't make head or tail.
MARION   Darling, did you hear what Mr Hop – er . . .
SIDNEY   Hopcroft.
MARION   Sidney, isn't it? Sidney was saying . . . ?
RONALD   What?
MARION   Darling, Sidney built this shelf on his own. He went out and measured the machine, got all his screws

14

and nails and heaven knows what and built this shelf himself.

RONALD Good Lord.

SIDNEY I've got some more shelves upstairs. For the bedside. And also, I've partitioned off part of the spare bedroom as a walk-in cupboard for the wife. And I'm just about to panel the landing with those knotty pine units, have you seen them?

MARION Those curtains are really the most insistent colour I've ever seen. They must just simply cry out to be drawn in the morning.

Jane sticks her head round the door

JANE Dear – it's Mr and Mrs Jackson.

SIDNEY Oh. Geoff and Eva, is it? Right, I'll be in to say hallo.

MARION Geoff and Eva Jackson?

SIDNEY Yes. Do you know them?

MARION Oh yes. Rather. Darling, it's Geoff and Eva Jackson.

RONALD Geoff and Eva who?

MARION The Jacksons.

RONALD Oh, Geoff and Eva Jackson. (*He goes and studies the washing machine*)

MARION That's nice, isn't it?

RONALD Yes?

JANE Are you coming in?

SIDNEY Yes, yes.

MARION Haven't seen them for ages.

JANE They've left the dog in the car.

SIDNEY Oh, good.

MARION Have they a dog?

JANE Yes.

MARION Oh, how lovely. We must see him.

JANE He's – very big . . .

SIDNEY Yes, well, lead on, dear.

Jane opens the door. A burst of conversation from the sitting-room.

15

Jane goes out. Sidney holds the door open for Marion, sees she is not following him and torn between his duties as a host, follows Jane off

We'll be in here. (*He closes the door*)

MARION   Ronnie . . .

RONALD   (*studying the washing machine*) Mm?

MARION   Come along, darling.

RONALD   I was just trying to work out how this thing does the ironing. Don't see it at all. Just rolls it into a ball.

MARION   Darling, do come on.

RONALD   I think that woman's got it wrong.

MARION   Darling . . .

RONALD   Um?

MARION   Make our excuses quite shortly, please.

RONALD   Had enough, have you?

MARION   We've left the boys . . .

RONALD   They'll be all right.

MARION   What's that man's name?

RONALD   Hopcroft, do you mean?

MARION   No, the other one.

RONALD   Oh, Potter, isn't it?

MARION   Well, I honestly don't think I can sit through many more of his jokes.

RONALD   I thought they were quite funny.

MARION   And I've never had quite such a small gin in my life. Completely drowned.

RONALD   Really? My Scotch was pretty strong.

MARION   That's only because she missed the glass with the soda water. Consider yourself lucky.

RONALD   I don't know about lucky. I shall probably have bloody rheumatism in the morning.

Sidney sticks his head round the door. Laughter and chatter behind him

SIDNEY   Er – Mrs Brewster-Wright, I wonder if you'd both . . .

MARION Oh, yes, we're just coming. We can't tear ourselves away from your divine kitchen, can we, Ronnie? (*Turning to Ronald, holding up the fingers of one hand and mouthing*) Five minutes.

RONALD Righto.

They all go out, closing the door

Silence

Jane enters with an empty bowl. She hurries to the cupboard and takes out a jumbo bag of crisps and pours them into the bowl. She is turning to leave when the door opens again and Sidney hurries in, looking a little fraught

SIDNEY Tonic water. We've run out.

JANE Tonic water. Down there in the cupboard.

SIDNEY Right.

JANE Do you think it's going all right?

SIDNEY Fine, fine. Now get back, get back there.

JANE (*as she goes*) Will you ask Lottie to stop eating all these crisps? Nobody else has had any.

Jane goes out closing the door behind her

Sidney searches first one cupboard, then another, but cannot find any tonic

SIDNEY Oh dear, oh dear.

Sidney hurries back to the party closing the door behind him. After a second Jane enters looking worried, closing the door behind her

She searches where Sidney has already searched. She finds nothing

JANE Oh. (*She wanders in rather aimless circles round the kitchen*)

Sidney enters with a glass with gin and a slice of lemon in it. He closes the door

SIDNEY Is it there?

JANE Yes, yes. Somewhere . . .

SIDNEY Well, come along. She's waiting.

17

JANE I've just – got to find it . . .

SIDNEY Oh dear, oh dear.

JANE I tidied them away somewhere.

SIDNEY Well, there was no point in tidying them away, was there? We're having a party.

JANE Well – it just looked – tidier. You go back in, I'll bring them.

SIDNEY Now that was your responsibility. We agreed buying the beverages was your department. I hope you haven't let us down.

JANE No. I'm sure I haven't.

SIDNEY Well, it's very embarrassing for me in the meanwhile, isn't it? Mrs Brewster-Wright is beginning to give me anxious looks.

JANE Oh.

SIDNEY Well then.

Sidney goes back in

Jane stands helplessly. She gives a little whimper of dismay. She is on the verge of tears. Then a sudden decision. She goes to a drawer, reaches to the back and brings out her housekeeping purse. She opens it and takes out some coins. She runs to the centre of the room and looks at the clock

JANE Nineteen-twenty-one. (*Hurried calculation*) Thirteen – fourteen – fifteen – sixteen – seventeen – eighteen – nineteen . . . seven-twenty-two. (*She hurries to the back door and opens it. She holds out her hand, takes a tentative step out and then a hasty step back again. She is again in a dilemma. She closes the back door. She goes to the cupboard just inside the door and, after rummaging about, she emerges holding a pair of men's large wellington boots in one hand and a pair of plimsolls in the other. Mentally tossing up between them, she returns the plimsolls to the cupboard. She slips off her own shoes and steps easily into the wellingtons. She puts her own shoes neatly in the cupboard and rummages again. She pulls out a large men's gardening raincoat. She holds it up, realizes it's better than nothing and puts it on. She hurries back to the centre of the room buttoning it as she does so*) Nineteen-twenty-four. (*She returns to the back door, opens it and steps out. It is evidently pelting down. She stands in the doorway holding up the collar of the coat and ineffectually trying to protect her hairdo from the rain with the other hand. Frantically*) Oh . . . (*She dives back into the cupboard and re-emerges with an old trilby hat. She looks at it in dismay. After a moment's struggle she puts it on and hurries back to the centre of the room*) Twenty-five.

Jane returns to the back door, hesitates for a second and then plunges out into the night, leaving the door only very slightly ajar. After a moment, Sidney returns still clutching the glass

SIDNEY   Jane? Jane! (*He looks round, puzzled*) Good gracious me. (*He peers around for her*)

Eva comes in. In her thirties, she makes no concessions in either manner or appearance

EVA   May I have a glass of water?
SIDNEY   Beg your pardon?
EVA   I have to take these. (*She holds out a couple of tablets enclosed in a sheet of tinfoil. She crosses to the back door and stands taking deep breaths of fresh air*)
SIDNEY   Oh, yes. There's a glass here somewhere, I think.
EVA   Thanks.
SIDNEY   (*finding a tumbler*) Here we are. (*He puts it down on the washing machine*)

Eva stands abstractedly staring ahead of her, tearing at the paper round the pills without any effort to open them. A pause. Sidney looks at her

Er . . .
EVA   What? Oh, thanks. (*She closes the back door and picks up the glass*)
SIDNEY   Not ill, I hope?
EVA   What?
SIDNEY   The pills. Not ill?
EVA   It depends what you mean by ill, doesn't it?

19

SIDNEY   Ah.

EVA   If you mean do they prevent me from turning into a raving lunatic, the answer's probably yes. (*She laughs somewhat bitterly*)

SIDNEY   (*laughing, too*) Raving lunatic, yes – (*he is none too certain of this lady*) – but then I always say, it helps to be a bit mad, doesn't it? I mean, we're all a bit mad. I'm a bit mad. (*Pause*) Yes. (*Pause*) It's a mad world, as they say.

EVA   (*surveying the pills in her hand which she has now opened*) Extraordinary to think that one's sanity can depend on these. Frightening, isn't it? (*She puts them both in her mouth and swallows the glass of water in one gulp*) Yuck. Alarming. Do you know I've been taking pills of one sort or another since I was eight years old. What chance does your body have? My husband tells me that even if I didn't need them, I'd still have to take them. My whole mentality is geared round swallowing tablets every three hours, twenty-four hours a day. I even have to set the alarm at night. You're looking at a mess. A wreck. (*She still holds the glass and is searching round absently as she speaks, for somewhere to put it*) Don't you sometimes long to be out of your body and free? Free just to float? I know I do. (*She opens the pedal bin with her foot and tosses the empty glass into it*) Thanks.

She puts the screwed up tinfoil into Sidney's hand and starts for the door. Sidney gawps at her. Eva pauses

My God, was that our car horn?

SIDNEY   When?

EVA   Just now.

SIDNEY   No, I don't think so.

EVA   If you do hear it, it's George.

SIDNEY   George?

EVA   Our dog.

SIDNEY   Oh, yes, of course.

EVA   We left him in the car, you see. We have to leave him in the car these days, he's just impossible. He's all right there, usually, but lately he's been getting bored and he's learnt to push the horn button with his nose. He just rests his nose on the steering-wheel, you see.

SIDNEY That's clever.

EVA Not all that clever. We've had the police out twice.

SIDNEY A bit like children, dogs.

EVA What makes you say that?

SIDNEY Need a bit of a firm hand now and again. Smack if they're naughty.

EVA You don't smack George, you negotiate terms.

SIDNEY Ah. (*He retrieves the glass from the waste bin*)

EVA He was only this big when we bought him, now he's grown into a sort of yak. When we took him in, he – my God was that me?

SIDNEY What?

EVA Did I put that glass in there?

SIDNEY Er – yes.

EVA My God, I knew it, I'm going mad. I am finally going mad. (*She goes to the door and opens it*)

Chatter is heard

Will you please tell my husband, if he drinks any more, I'm walking home.

SIDNEY Well, I think that might be better coming from you as his wife.

EVA (*laughing*) You really think he'd listen to me? He doesn't even know I'm here. As far as he's concerned, my existence ended the day he married me. I'm just an embarrassing smudge on a marriage licence.

Eva goes out, closing the door

SIDNEY Ah. (*He puts the glass on the washing machine and finds Jane's discarded shoes on the floor. He picks them up, stares at them and places them on the draining-board. Puzzled, he crosses to the back door and calls out into the night*) Jane! (*He listens. No reply*)

21

Marion comes in

Jane!

MARION   I say . . .

SIDNEY   Rain . . . (*He holds out his hand by way of demonstration, then closes the back door*)

MARION   Oh, yes, dreadful. I say, I think you dashed away with my glass.

SIDNEY   Oh, I'm so sorry. (*Handing it to her*) Here.

MARION   Thank you. I was getting terribly apprehensive in case it had gone into your washing machine. (*She sips the drink*) Oh, that's lovely. Just that teeny bit stronger. You know what I mean. Not too much tonic . . .

SIDNEY   No, well . . .

MARION   Perfect.

SIDNEY   Actually, that's neat gin, that is.

MARION   Oh, good heavens! So it is. What are you trying to do to me? I can see we're going to have to keep an eye on you. Mr – er . . .

SIDNEY   No, no. You're safe enough with me.

MARION   Yes, I'm sure . . .

SIDNEY   The mistletoe's in there.

MARION   Well, what are we waiting for? Lead on, Mr – er . . . (*She ushers him in front of her*)

SIDNEY   Follow me.

Sidney goes through the door

MARION   (*as she turns to close it, looking at her watch*) My God.

Marion goes out and closes the door

A pause

Jane arrives at the back door still in her hat, coat and boots. She is soaking wet. She carries a carton of tonic waters. She rattles the back door knob but she has locked herself out. She knocks gently then louder, but no-one hears her. She rattles the knob again, pressing her face up against the glass. We see her mouth opening and shutting but no sound. Eventually, she gives up and hurries away. After a second, Sidney returns. He has the crisp bowl which is again empty. He is about to refill it when he pauses and looks round the kitchen, puzzled and slightly annoyed. He goes to the back door and opens it

SIDNEY   Jane! Jane!

Sidney turns up his jacket collar and runs out, leaving the door ajar

As soon as Sidney has gone, the doorbell chimes. There is a pause, then it chimes again, several times

   Ronald enters from the sitting-room

RONALD   I say, old boy, I think someone's at your front – oh. (*He sees the empty room and the open back door*)

Ronald turns and goes back into the room

No, he seems to have gone out. I suppose we'd better . . . (*His voice cuts off as he closes the door*)

The doorbell chimes once more.

   Sidney returns, closing the back door. He finds a towel and dabs his face and hair

SIDNEY   Dear oh dear. (*He shakes his head and returns to his crisps. Suddenly, the living-room door bursts open and Jane enters hurriedly in her strange garb, her boots squelching. She shuts the door behind her and stands against it, shaking and exhausted*)

Sidney turns and throws the bag of crisps into the air in his astonishment

JANE   Oh, my goodness.
SIDNEY   What are you doing?
JANE   Oh.
SIDNEY   (*utterly incredulous*) What do you think you're doing?
JANE   (*still breathless*) I went – I went out – to get the tonic. (*She puts a carton of tonic waters on the table*)
SIDNEY   Like that?
JANE   I couldn't find – I didn't want . . .

23

SIDNEY   You went out – and came in again, like that?

JANE   I thought I'd just slip out the back to the off-licence and slip in again. But I locked myself out. I had to come in the front.

SIDNEY   But who let you in?

JANE   (*in a whisper*) Mr Brewster-Wright.

SIDNEY   Mr Brewster-Wright? Mr Brewster-Wright let you in like that?

Jane nods

What did he say?

JANE   I don't think he recognized me.

SIDNEY   I'm not surprised.

JANE   I couldn't look at him. I just ran straight past him and right through all of them and into here.

SIDNEY   Like that?

JANE   Yes.

SIDNEY   But what did they say?

JANE   They didn't say anything. They just stopped talking and stared and I ran through them. I couldn't very well . . .

SIDNEY   You'll have to go back in there and explain.

JANE   No, I couldn't.

SIDNEY   Of course you must.

JANE   Sidney, I don't think I can face them.

SIDNEY   You can't walk through a respectable cocktail party, the hostess, dressed like that without an apology.

JANE   (*on the verge of tears again*) I couldn't.

SIDNEY   (*furious*) You take off all that – and you go back in there and explain.

JANE   (*with a wail*) I just want to go to bed.

SIDNEY   Well, you cannot go to bed. Not at nineteen-forty-seven. Now, take off that coat.

Jane squelches to the cupboard

Ronald opens the kitchen door. He is talking over his shoulder as he comes in, carrying a glass of Scotch

24

RONALD Well, I think I'd better, I mean . . .

JANE Oh, no.

Jane has had no time to unbutton her coat. Rather than face Ronald, she rushes out of the back door hatless, abandoning her headgear in the middle of the kitchen table

Sidney, trying to stop Jane, lunges after her vainly. The door slams behind her. Sidney stands with his back to it

RONALD (*in the doorway, having caught a glimpse of violent activity, but unsure what*) Ah, there you are, old chap.

SIDNEY Oh, hallo. Hallo.

RONALD Just popped out, did you?

SIDNEY Yes, just popped out.

RONALD Well – something rather odd. Someone at the door just now. Little short chap. Hat, coat, boots and bottles. Just stamped straight through. You catch a glimpse of him?

SIDNEY Oh, him.

RONALD Belong here, does he? I mean . . .

SIDNEY Oh, yes

RONALD Ah. Well, as long as you know about him. Might have been after your silver. I mean, you never know. Not these days.

SIDNEY No, indeed. No, he – he was from the off-licence. (*He shows Ronald the carton*)

RONALD Really?

SIDNEY Brought round our order of tonic, you see.

Ronald stares at the hat on the table. Sidney notices and picks it up

Silly fellow. Left his hat. (*He picks up the hat, walks to the back door, opens it and throws out the hat. He closes the door*)

RONALD Not the night to forget your hat.

SIDNEY No, indeed.

RONALD (*sitting at the table*) Mind you, frankly, he didn't look all there to me. Wild eyed. That's what made me think . . .

25

SIDNEY Quite right.

RONALD Ought to get him to come round the back, you know. Take a tip from me. Once you let tradesmen into the habit of using your front door, you might as well move out, there and then.

SIDNEY Well, quite. In my own particular business, I always insist that my staff . . .

RONALD Oh, yes, of course. I was forgetting you're a – you're in business yourself, aren't you?

SIDNEY Well, in a small way at the moment. My wife and I. I think I explained . . .

RONALD Yes, of course. And doing very well.

SIDNEY Well, for a little general stores, you know. Mustn't grumble.

RONALD Good to hear someone's making the grade.

SIDNEY These days.

RONALD Quite. (*He picks up the booklet and looks at it*)

A pause

SIDNEY I know this isn't perhaps the moment, I mean it probably isn't the right moment, but none the less, I hope you've been giving a little bit of thought to our chat. The other day. If you've had a moment.

RONALD Chat? Oh, yes – chat. At the bank? Well, yes, it's – probably not, as you say, the moment but, as I said then – and this is still off the cuff you understand – I think the bank could probably see their way to helping you out.

SIDNEY Ah well, that's wonderful news. You see, as I envisage it, once I can get the necessary loan, that means I can put in a definite bid for the adjoining site – which hasn't inci- dentally come on to the market. I mean, as I said this is all purely through personal contacts.

RONALD Quite so, yes.

SIDNEY I mean the site value alone – just taking it as a site – you follow me?

RONALD Oh, yes.

SIDNEY But it is a matter of striking while the iron's hot – before it goes off the boil . . .

RONALD Mmm . . .

SIDNEY I mean, in this world it's dog eat dog, isn't it? No place for sentiment. Not in business. I mean, all right, so on occasions you can scratch mine. I'll scratch yours . . .

RONALD Beg your pardon?

SIDNEY Tit for tat. But when the chips are down it's every man for himself and blow you Jack, I regret to say . .

RONALD Exactly.

The sitting-room door opens. Geoffrey enters. Mid-thirties. Good-looking, confident, easy-going. He carries a glass of Scotch

GEOFFREY Ah. Is there a chance of sanctuary here?

RONALD Hallo.

GEOFFREY Like Dick Potter's harem in there.

SIDNEY Dick still at it?

GEOFFREY Yes. Keeping the ladies amused with jokes . . .

RONALD Is he? Oh, dear. I'd better – in a minute . . .

GEOFFREY You'll never stop him. Is he always like that? Or does he just break out at Christmas?

SIDNEY Oh, no. Dick's a great laugh all the year round . . .

GEOFFREY Is he?

RONALD You don't say?

SIDNEY He's a very fascinating character, is Dick. I thought you'd be interested to meet him. I mean, so's she. In her way. Very colourful. They're both teachers, you know. But he's very involved with youth work of all types. He takes these expeditions off to the mountains. A party of lads. Walks in Scotland. That sort of thing. Wonderful man with youngsters . . .

RONALD Really?

SIDNEY Got a lot of facets.

RONALD Got a good-looking wife . . .

SIDNEY Lottie? Yes, she's a fine-looking woman. Always very well turned out . . .

27

GEOFFREY Yes, she seems to have turned out quite well.

SIDNEY She does the same as him with girls . . .

RONALD I beg your pardon?

SIDNEY Hiking and so on. With the Brownies, mainly.

RONALD Oh, I see.

GEOFFREY Oh.

Pause

RONALD Better join the Brownies, then, hadn't we? (*He laughs*)

SIDNEY (*at length; laughing*) Yes, I like that. Better join the Brownies. (*He laughs*) You must tell that to Dick. That would tickle Dick no end.

GEOFFREY (*after a pause*) Nice pair of legs.

RONALD Yes.

SIDNEY Dick?

GEOFFREY His wife.

SIDNEY Lottie? Oh, yes. Mind you, I don't think I've really noticed them . . .

GEOFFREY Usually, when they get to about that age, they tend to go a bit flabby round here. (*He pats his thigh*) But she's very trim . . .

RONALD Trim, oh yes.

GEOFFREY Nice neat little bum . . .

SIDNEY Ah.

RONALD Has she? Hadn't seen that.

GEOFFREY I was watching her, getting up and stretching out for the crisps. Very nice indeed.

RONALD Oh, well, I'll keep an eye out.

Pause

SIDNEY That'll be the hiking . . .

GEOFFREY What?

SIDNEY (*tapping his thighs; somewhat self-consciously*) This – you know. That'll be the hiking . . .

RONALD Yes. (*After a pause*) How did you happen to see those?

GEOFFREY What?

28

RONALD   Her . . . (*He slaps his thighs*) I mean when I saw her
just now she had a great big woolly – thing on. Down to
here.

GEOFFREY   Oh, you can get around that.

RONALD   Really?

GEOFFREY   I've been picking imaginary peanuts off the floor
round her feet all evening.

Ronald laughs uproariously. Sidney joins in, a little out of his depth

RONALD   You'll have to watch this fellow, you know.

SIDNEY   Oh, yes?

RONALD   Don't leave your wife unattended if he's around.

SIDNEY   Oh, no?

RONALD   Lock her away . . .

SIDNEY   (*getting the joke at last and laughing*) Ah-ha! Yes . . .

Jane suddenly appears outside the back door, peering in

Sidney waves her away with urgent gestures

GEOFFREY   Still raining, is it?

SIDNEY   (*holding out his hand*) Yes. Yes.

RONALD   I'll tell you what I've been meaning to ask you . . .

GEOFFREY   What's that?

RONALD   Remember that party we were both at – during the
summer – Malcolm Freebody's . . .?

GEOFFREY   When was this?

RONALD   Eva – your wife was off sick . . .

GEOFFREY   That's nothing unusual.

RONALD   I remember it because you were making tremendous
headway with some woman that Freebody was using on his
public relations thing . . .

GEOFFREY   Was I?

RONALD   Blonde. Sort of blonde.

GEOFFREY   (*a short thought*) Binnie.

RONALD   Binnie, was it?

GEOFFREY   Binnie something. I think . . .

29

RONALD   Make out all right, did you?

GEOFFREY   Well – you know . . .

RONALD   Really?

GEOFFREY   You have no idea. Absolute little cracker. Married
to a steward on P. and O. Hadn't seen him for eight months
. . .

RONALD   (*chuckling*) Good Lord . . .

SIDNEY   Ah – ha – oh – ha – ha-ha. (*And other noises of sexual
approval*)

The others look at him

GEOFFREY   What have you done with yours? Buried her in the
garden?

SIDNEY   (*guiltily*) What? No, no. She's about. Somewhere.

GEOFFREY   Wish I could lose mine, sometimes. Her and that
dog. There's hardly room for me in the flat – I mean
between the two of them, they have completely reduced that
flat to rubble. I mean I'm very fond of her, bless her, she's
a lovely girl – but she just doesn't know what it's all about.
She really doesn't.

RONALD   Maybe. I still think you're pretty lucky with Eva
. . .

GEOFFREY   Why's that?

RONALD   Well, she must have a jolly good idea by now about
your – er . . .

GEOFFREY   Yes. I should imagine she probably has . . .

RONALD   Well, there you are . . .

GEOFFREY   Oh now, come off it. Nonsense. She chooses to live
with me, she lives by my rules. I mean we've always made
that perfectly clear. She lives her life to a certain extent; I
live mine, do what I like within reason. It's the only way
to do it . . .

SIDNEY   Good gracious.

RONALD   I wish you'd have a chat with Marion. Convince her.

GEOFFREY   Any time. Pleasure.

RONALD   Yes, well, perhaps not – on second thoughts.

GEOFFREY   No, seriously. Any man, it doesn't matter who he is – you, me, anyone – (*pointing at Sidney*) – him. They've just got to get it organized. I mean face it, there's just too much good stuff wandering around simply crying out for it for you not . . .

The living-room door opens. Eva appears. Behind, Dick Potter still in full flow, laughing

(*To Sidney, altering his tone immediately*) Anyway, I think that would be a good idea. Don't you?

EVA   (*coolly*) Are you all proposing to stay out here all night?

SIDNEY   Oh, dear. We seem to have neglected the ladies.

EVA   Neglected? We thought we'd been bloody well abandoned.

GEOFFREY   Can't manage without us, you see.

EVA   We can manage perfectly well, thank you. It just seemed to us terribly rude, that's all.

GEOFFREY   Oh, good God . . .

EVA   Anyway. Your jolly friends are leaving.

SIDNEY   Oh, really. Dick and Lottie? I'd better pop out and see them off, then. Excuse me . . .

Sidney goes off to the sitting-room

EVA   And, darling, unless you want to see our car towed away again, horn blazing – we'd better get our coats.

GEOFFREY   He's not at it again . . .

EVA   Past his supper time . . .

GEOFFREY   Oh, honestly, Eva . . .

EVA   Don't honestly Eva me, darling. He's your dog.

GEOFFREY   What do you mean, he's my dog?

EVA   (*sweetly*) Your house, your dog, your car, your wife – we all belong to you, darling – we all expect to be provided for. Now are you coming please?

Ronald smiles

And your wife is looking slightly less than pleased, I might tell you.

31

Ronald's smile fades

Eva goes out

RONALD Oh. (*He looks at his watch*) I suppose I'd better er
. . .

GEOFFREY Oh. Ronnie. By the way . . .

RONALD Mmmm?

GEOFFREY I wondered if you heard anything on the grapevine
about the new building Harrison's having put up . . .

RONALD Oh, this new shopping complex of his.

GEOFFREY Has he got anyone yet?

RONALD What, you mean in your line?

GEOFFREY Yes. Has he settled on an architect? Or is it still
open?

RONALD Well, as far as I know, it's still wide open. I mean,
it's still a gleam in his eye as far as I know.

GEOFFREY Well. If you get a chance to put in a word. I know
you're fairly thick with him.

RONALD Yes, of course. I'll mention it, if the topic comes up.
I mean, I'm sure you could do as a good job as anyone.

GEOFFREY Look, I can design, standing on my head, any
building that Harrison's likely to want.

RONALD Yes, well, as I say, I'll mention it.

GEOFFREY I'd be grateful . . .

Marion comes in

RONALD Ah.

MARION All right, darling, we're off . . .

RONALD Right.

MARION Had a nice time out here?

RONALD Oh, yes, grand.

MARION Good. As long as you have . . .

Ronald goes off into the living-room

This really is a simply loathsome little house. I mean how
can people live in them. I mean, Geoff, you're an architect,

you must be able to tell me. How do people come to design these sort of monstrosities in the first place, let alone persuade people to live in them?

GEOFFREY Well. . .

MARION Oh, God. Now he's going to tell me he designed it.

GEOFFREY No. I didn't do it. They're designed like this mainly because of cost and people who are desperate for somewhere to live aren't particularly choosey.

MARION Oh, come. Nobody can be this desperate.

GEOFFREY You'd be surprised.

MARION Anyway, it's been lovely to see you. It's been ages. You must come up and see us . . .

Sidney and Ronald, now in his overcoat and carrying Marion's coat, return

RONALD Darling . . .

MARION Sidney, we've had a simply lovely time. Now some time you must come up and see us – and your wife, that's if you ever find her. . .

SIDNEY Yes, yes indeed . . .

They all go out, chattering, closing the door

Silence

After a pause, Sidney returns. He closes the door

(*Rubbing his hands together*) Hah! (*He smiles. Quite pleased. He takes up his drink and sips it. He munches a crisp*)

There is a knock at the back door – rather tentative. It is Jane

Sidney frowns. His concentration is disturbed

Just a minute. (*He opens the back door*)

Jane falls in – a sodden mass

(*Recoiling*) My word.

JANE I saw them leaving.

33

SIDNEY   Yes. All gone now. They said for me to say good-bye
  to you.

JANE   Oh.

SIDNEY   Where have you been?

JANE   In the garden. Where else? Where do you think?

SIDNEY   Oh – I don't know. You might have been for a stroll.

JANE   In this?

SIDNEY   Oh. Still raining, is it?

JANE   Yes. (*Pause*) Sidney, if you'd only explained to them –
  I could've – I mean I've been out there for ages. I'm soaking
  . . .

SIDNEY   Yes. Well, your behaviour made things very difficult.
  Explanations, that is. What could I say?

JANE   You could have explained.

SIDNEY   So could you. It was really up to you, wasn't it?

JANE   Yes, I know but – I just thought that you might have
  – that you would've been . . . (*She gives up*)

Jane starts to peel off her things

SIDNEY   All went off rather satisfactorily, anyway. . .

JANE   (*emptying a wellington boot into the sink*) Good – I'm
  glad . . .

SIDNEY   So am I. I mean these people just weren't anybody.
  They are people in the future who can be very, very useful
  to us . . .

JANE   (*emptying the other boot*) Yes . . .

SIDNEY   Now, you mustn't do that, Jane. You really mustn't.
  You see, you get yourself all worked up. And then what
  happens?

JANE   Yes.

SIDNEY   Right. Enough said. All forgotten, eh? (*Pause*) Oh
  dear . . .

JANE   What?

SIDNEY   We never got round to playing any of our games, did
  we?

JANE   No.

SIDNEY In all the excitement. Never mind. Another year. Well. I think I'll have a look at television. Should be something. Christmas Eve. Usually is. Coming in, are you?

JANE In a minute ...

SIDNEY Right then.

Sidney goes out closing the door

Jane stands. She sniffs. She has finished putting away her things. Her eye lights on the dirty things scattered about. She picks up a glass or so and puts them in the sink. She picks up the damp cloth and wipes first where the glasses were standing and then slowly, in wider and wider circles, till she has turned it, once more, into a full-scale cleaning operation. As she cleans she seems to relax. Softly at first, then louder, she is heard to sing happily to herself, and –

the CURTAIN *falls*

Act Two

Geoffrey and Eva Jackson's kitchen in their fourth-floor flat. This Christmas

One door leads to the sitting-room, another into a walk-in cupboard. The room gives an immediate impression of untidiness. It is a room continually lived in, unlike the Hopcrofts' immaculate ship's bridge. While it gives signs that the owners have a certain taste for the trendy homespun in both equipment and furnishings, some of the equipment, particularly the gas stove, has seen better days. Besides the stove, the room contains a table (natural scrubbed wood), kitchen chairs (natural scrubbed wood), a chest of drawers (natural scrubbed wood) and a fridge and sink

When the CURTAIN rises Eva, unmade-up, unkempt and baggy-eyed, sits at the table in her dressing-gown. She is writing with a stub of pencil in a notepad. Whatever it is, it is difficult to word. She and the floor around her are ringed with screwed-up pieces of paper. In front of her is an open Scotch bottle. After a minute she tears out the page she has been working on, screws that up as well, and tosses it on the floor to join the others. She starts again

A door slams. From the sitting-room comes the sound of a large dog barking. Eva looks up alarmed, consults her watch, gives a moan, and quickly closes the notepad to cover up what she has been writing. Geoffrey's voice is heard off.

GEOFFREY (*off*) Darling? Eva – Eva! Quiet, George!

  Geoffrey backs in from the sitting-room

George is still barking with wild glee

  George! That's enough, George! Don't be silly, boy. Sit, George. Sit, boy. At once. That's a good boy. Sit. Good George. Good . . .

George has quietened. Geoffrey goes to close the door. George barks with fresh vigour

George . . .! (*Giving up*) Oh, all right, suit yourself. (*He closes the door, turning to face Eva for the first time*) Hallo, darling. (*He gives her a kiss as he passes*)

Eva hardly seems to notice. Instead, she sits fiddling with one of her pieces of screwed-up paper. Her face is a tense blank

God, I need a drink. You want a drink? (*Without waiting for a reply, he takes the Scotch, finds a glass and pours himself a drink*) You want one? No? (*He puts the bottle back on the table and drinks*) Cheers. I think we're running into some sort of trouble with the Harrison job. Helluva day. Would you believe I could spend two months explaining to them exactly how to assemble that central-dome. I go along this morning, they're trying to put a bloody great pillar up the middle, straight through the fountain. I said to them, 'Listen, you promise to put it up as you're told to – I promise it'll stay up, all right?' I now have to tell Harrison that his super Shopperdrome that he thought was only going to cost so much is going to finish up at twice that. He is not going to be pleased. No, I think I'm in trouble unless I can . . . Oh well, what the hell, it's Christmas. (*Going to the window*) You know, I think it's going to snow. By Boxing Day, that site'll be under six foot of slush, mark my words. That'll put us another six months behind. (*Returning from the window*) Why didn't I pick something simple? (*Seeing the screwed-up paper*) What've you been up to? (*He tries to take Eva's writing pad*)

Eva clings to the pad. Geoffrey shrugs, moves away, then turns and looks at her

You all right? You're still in your dressing-gown, did you know? Eva? Are you still thinking about this morning? I phoned you at lunch, you know. Were you out? Eva? Oh, come on, darling, we talked it over, didn't we? We were up till four o'clock this morning talking it over. You agreed. You did more than agree. I mean, it was your idea. And you're right. Believe me, darling, you were right. We can't

37

go on. Sooner or later one of us has got to do something really positive for once in our lives – for both our sakes. And it's absolutely true that the best thing that could happen to you and me, at this point in our lives, is for me to go and live with Sally. You were absolutely right. You know I was thinking on the way home – I nipped in for a quick one, that's why I'm a bit late – I was thinking, this could actually work out terribly well. If we're adult about it, I mean. Don't behave like lovesick kids or something. Sally and I will probably get somewhere together – and by that time you'll probably have got yourself fixed up – we could still see each other, you know. What I'm really saying is, let's not go through all that nonsense – all that good-bye, I never want to see you again bit. Because I do want to see you again. I always will. I mean, five years. We're not going to throw away five years, are we? Eva? Eva, if you're sitting there blaming yourself for this in any way, don't. It's me, love, it's all me. It's just I'm – okay, I'm weak, as you put it. I'm unstable. It's something lacking in me, I know. I mean, other men don't have this trouble. Other men can settle down and be perfectly happy with one woman for the rest of their lives. And that's a wonderful thing. Do you think I don't envy that? (*Banging the table*) God, how I envy them that. I mean, do you really think I enjoy living out my life like some sexual Flying Dutchman? Eva, please – please try and see my side just a little, will you? Look, it's Christmas Eve. The day after Boxing Day, I promise – I'll just clear everything of mine that you don't need out of the flat. That way, you can forget I even existed, if that's what you want. But can't we try, between us to make the next couple of days . . . (*He breaks off*) Did I say it's Christmas Eve? Haven't we got some people coming round? Yes, surely we . . . What time did we ask them for? (*He looks at his watch*) Oh, my God. You didn't remember to put them off by any chance, did you? No. Well then . . . Have we got anything to drink in the house? Apart from this? (*He holds up the bottle of Scotch*)

Oh well, we'll have that for a start. Now then . . . (*He finds a tray, puts it on the table and puts the Scotch bottle on the table*) What else have we got? (*He rummages in the cupboards*) Brandy. That'll do. Bottle of coke. Aha, what's this? Tonic wine? Who's been drinking tonic wine? Is that you? Eva? Oh, for heaven's sake, Eva – you've made your point, now snap out of it, will you? We have lots of people coming round who were due five minutes ago. Now come on . . . (*He looks at her and sighs*) O.K. I get the message. O.K. There is no help or co-operation to be expected from you tonight, is that it? All systems shut down again, have they? All right. All right. It won't be the first time – don't worry. (*He returns to his hunt for bottles*) I mean it's not as if you're particularly famous as a gracious hostess, is it? It hasn't been unheard of for you to disappear to bed in the middle of a party and be found later reading a book. (*Producing a couple more bottles – gin and sherry*) I should think our friends will be a little disappointed if you do put in an appearance. (*Finding an assortment of glasses*) When I say our friends, perhaps I should say yours. I will remind you that, so far as I can remember, all the people coming tonight come under the heading of your friends and not mine. And if I'm left to entertain them tonight because you choose to opt out, I shall probably finish up being very, very rude to them. Is that clear? Right. You have been warned. Yes, I know. You're very anxious, aren't you, that I should go and work for the up and coming Mr Hopcroft? So is up and coming Mr Hopcroft. But I can tell you both, here and now, I have no intention of helping to perpetrate his squalid little developments. What I lack in morals – I make up in ethics.

Geoffrey stamps out into the sitting-room with the tray

(*Off, as George starts barking again*) George – no, this is not for you. Get down. I said get down. (*There is a crash as of a bottle coming off the tray*) Oh, really – this damn dog – get out of it . . .

Geoffrey returns with a couple of old coffee-cups which he puts in the sink

That room is like a very untidy cesspit. (*He finds a dish cloth*) One quick drink, that's all they're getting. Then it's happy Christmas and out they bloody well go.

Geoffrey goes out again. He takes with him the dish cloth

Eva opens her notepad and continues with her note

Geoffrey returns. He still has the cloth. In the other hand he has a pile of bits of broken dog biscuit

Half-chewed biscuit. Why does he only chew half of them, can you tell me that? (*He desposits the bits in the waste bin. He is about to exit again, then pauses*) Eva? Eva – I'm being very patient. Very patient indeed. But in a minute I really do believe I'm going to lose my temper. And we know what happens then, don't we? I will take a swing at you and then you will feel hard done by and, by way of reprisal, will systematically go round and smash everything in the flat. And come tomorrow breakfast time, there will be the familiar sight of the three of us, you, me and George, trying to eat our meals off our one surviving plate. Now, Eva, *please* . . .

The doorbell rings. George starts barking

Oh, my God. Here's the first of them. (*Calling*) George. Now, Eva, go to bed now, please. Don't make things any more embarrassing. (*As he goes out*) George, will you be quiet.

Geoffrey goes out. The door closes. Silence

Eva opens her notepad, finishes her note and tears it out. She pushes the clutter on the table to one side slightly. She goes to a drawer and produces a kitchen knife. She returns to the table and pins the note forcibly to it with the knife. She goes to the window

Geoffrey returns

Barking and chattering are heard in the background – two voices. Eva stands motionless, looking out

(*Calling back*) He's all right. He's quite harmless. Bark's worse than his bite. (*He closes the door*) It would be the bloody Hopcrofts, wouldn't it? Didn't think they'd miss out. And that lift's broken down, would you believe it? (*Finding a bottle-opener in a drawer*) Every Christmas. Every Christmas, isn't it? Eva, come on, love, for heaven's sake.

Geoffrey goes out, closing the door

Eva opens the window. She inhales the cold fresh air. After a second, she climbs uncertainly on to the window ledge. She stands giddily, staring down and clutching on to the frame

The door opens, chatter, Geoffrey returns, carrying a glass

(*Calling behind him*) I'll get you a clean one, I'm terribly sorry. I'm afraid the cook's on holiday. (*He laughs*)

The Hopcrofts' laughter is heard. Geoffrey closes the door

Don't think we can have washed these glasses since the last party. This one certainly didn't pass the Jane Hopcroft Good Housekeeping Test, anyway. (*He takes a dish cloth from the sink and wipes the glass rather casually*) I sometimes think that woman must spend . . . Eva! What are you doing?

Eva, who is now feeling sick with vertigo, moans

Eva! Eva – that's a good girl. Down. Come down – come down – that's a good girl – down. Come on . . . (*He reaches Eva*) That's it. Easy. Come on, I've got you. Down you come. That's it.

He eases Eva gently back into the room. She stands limply. He guides her inert body to a chair

Come on, sit down here. That's it. Darling, darling, what were you trying to do? What on earth made you want to

41

. . .? What was the point of that, what were you trying to prove? I mean . . . (*He sees the note and the knife for the first time*) What on earth's this? (*He reads it*) Oh, no. Eva, you mustn't think of . . . I mean, what do you mean, a burden to everyone? Who said you were a burden? I never said you were a burden . . .

During the above, Eva picks up the bread-knife, looks at it, then at one of the kitchen drawers. She rises, unseen by Geoffrey, crosses to the drawer and, half opening it, wedges the knife inside so the point sticks out. She measures out a run and turns to face the knife. Geoffrey, still talking, is now watching her absently. Eva works up speed and then takes a desperate run at the point of the knife. Geoffrey, belatedly realizing what she's up to, rushes forward, intercepts her and re-seats her

Eva, now, for heaven's sake! Come on . . . (*He studies her nervously*) Look, I'm going to phone the doctor. I'll tell him you're very upset and overwrought. (*He backs away and nearly impales himself on the knife. He grabs it*) He can probably give you something to calm you down a bit.

The doorbell rings

Oh God, somebody else. Now, I'm going to phone the doctor. I'll just be two minutes, all right? Now, you sit there. Don't move, just sit there like a good girl. (*Opening the door and calling off*) Would you mind helping yourselves? I just have to make one phone call . . .

Geoffrey goes out

Silence. Eva finishes another note. A brief one. She tears it out and weights it down, this time with a tin of dog food which happens to be on the table. She gazes round, surveying the kitchen. She stares at the oven. She goes to it and opens it, looking inside thoughtfully. She reaches inside and removes a casserole dish, opens the lid, wrinkles her nose and carries it to the draining-board. Returning to the oven, she removes three shelves and various other odds and ends that seem to have accumulated in there. It is a very dirty oven. She looks at her hands, now grimy, goes to the kitchen drawer and fetches a nearly clean tea towel. Folding it carefully, she lays it on the floor of the oven. She lies down and sticks her head inside, as if trying it for size. She is apparently dreadfully uncomfortable. She wriggles about to find a satisfactory position

The door opens quietly and Jane enters

The hubbub outside has now died down to a gentle murmur so not much noise filters through. Jane carries rather carefully two more glasses she considers dirty. She closes the door. She looks round the kitchen but sees no-one. She crosses, rather furtively, to the sink and rinses the glasses. Eva throws an oven tray on to the floor with a clatter. Jane, startled, takes a step back and gives a little squeak. Eva, equally startled, tries to sit up in the oven and hits her head with a clang on the remaining top shelf

JANE (*recovering*) Mrs Jackson, are you all right? You shouldn't be on the cold floor in your condition, you know. You should be in bed. Surely? Here . . .

She helps Eva to her feet and steers her back to the table

Now, you sit down here. Don't you worry about that oven now. That oven can wait. You clean it later. No point in damaging your health for an oven, is there? Mind you, I know just what you feel like, though. You suddenly get that urge, don't you? You say, I must clean that oven if it kills me. I shan't sleep, I shan't eat till I've cleaned that oven. It haunts you. I know just that feeling. I'll tell you what I'll do. Never say I'm not a good neighbour – shall I have a go at it for you? How would that be? Would you mind? I mean, it's no trouble for me. I quite enjoy it, actually – and you'd do the same for me, wouldn't you? Right. That's settled. No point in wasting time, let's get down to it. Now then, what are we going to need? Bowl of water, got any oven cleaner, have you? Never mind, we'll find it – I hope you're not getting cold, you look very peaky. (*Hunting under the sink*) Now then, oven cleaner? Have we got any? Well, if we haven't, we'll just have to use our old friend Mr Vim, won't we? (*She rummages*)

The door opens: Geoffrey enters and goes to Eva. Conversation is heard in the background

GEOFFREY   Darling, listen, it looks as if I've got . . . (*Seeing Jane*) Oh.

JANE   Hallo, there.

GEOFFREY   Oh, hallo – anything you – want?

JANE   I'm just being a good neighbour, that's all. Have you by any chance got an apron I could borrow?

GEOFFREY   (*rather bewildered, pointing to the chair*) Er – yes – there.

JANE   Oh, yes. (*Putting it on*) Couldn't see it for looking.

GEOFFREY   Er – what are you doing?

JANE   Getting your oven ready for tomorrow, that's what I'm doing.

GEOFFREY   For what?

JANE   For your Christmas dinner. What else do you think for what?

GEOFFREY   Yes, well, are you sure. . .?

JANE   Don't you worry about me. (*She bustles around singing loudly, collecting cleaning things and a bowl of water*)

GEOFFREY   (*over this, irritated*) Oh. Darling – Eva, look I've phoned the doctor but he's not there. He's apparently out on a call somewhere and the fool of a woman I spoke to has got the address and no number. It'll be quicker for me to try and catch him there than sitting here waiting for him to come back. Now, I'll be about ten minutes, that's all. You'll be all right, will you?

JANE   Don't you fret. I'll keep an eye on her. (*She puts on a rubber glove*)

GEOFFREY   Thank you. (*He studies the immobile Eva. On a sudden inspiration, crosses to the kitchen drawer and starts taking out the knives. He scours the kitchen, gathering up the sharp implements*)

Jane watches him, puzzled

(*By way of explanation*) People downstairs are having a big dinner-party. Promised to lend them some stuff.

JANE Won't they need forks?
GEOFFREY No. No forks. They're Muslims. (*As he goes to the door*) Ten minutes.

The doorbell rings

JANE There's somebody.
GEOFFREY The Brewster-Wrights, probably.
JANE Oh . . .

Geoffrey goes out, the dog barking as he does so, until the door is closed

Hark at that dog of yours. Huge, isn't he? Like a donkey – huge. Do you know what Dick's bought him? Dick Potter? He's bought George a Christmas present. One of those rubber rings. You know the ones you throw in the air. One of those. He loves it. He's been running up and down your hallway out there – Dick throwing it, him trying to catch it. But he's really wonderful with dogs, Dick. He really understands them. Do you know he nearly became a dog handler only he didn't have his proper eyesight. But he knows how to treat them. Doesn't matter what sort of dog it is . . . He knows all their ways. (*Turning to the oven*) Now then – oh, this is going to be a big one, isn't it? Dear oh dear. Never mind. Where there's a will. (*Removing the tea towel from the oven*) You haven't been trying to clean it with this, have you? You'll never clean it with this. Good old elbow grease – that's the way. (*She sets to work, her head almost inside the oven*) Shall I tell you something – Sidney would get so angry if he heard me saying this – but I'd far sooner be down here on the floor, on my knees in the oven – than out there, talking. Isn't that terrible. But I'm never at ease, really, at parties. I don't enjoy drinking, you see. I'd just

45

as soon be out here, having a natter with you. (*She starts to sing cheerily as she works, her voice booming round the oven*)

During this, Eva rises, opens the cupboard, pulls out a tin box filled with first-aid things and searches through the contents. Eventually, she finds a white cylindrical cardboard pill box which is what she's looking for. She goes to the sink with it and runs herself a glass of water. She opens the box, takes out a couple of small tablets and puts the box back on the draining-board. She swallows one tablet with a great deal of difficulty and water. The same with the second. She leaves the tap running, pulls the cotton-wool out of the box – and the rest of the pills rattle down the drain. Eva tries desperately to save some with her finger before they can disappear, turning off the tap. This proving ineffective, she tries with a fork

The door opens. Barking and chatter are heard. Sidney enters

SIDNEY   Hallo, hallo. Where's everyone gone, then . . . (*Seeing Jane*) Dear oh dear. I just can't believe it. I just can't believe my eyes. You can't be at it again. What are you doing?

JANE   She's under the weather. She needs a hand.

SIDNEY   Do you realize that's your best dress?

JANE   Oh, bother my best dress.

SIDNEY   Mr and Mrs Brewster-Wright have arrived, you know. Ron and Marion. I hope they don't chance to see you down there. (*Turning to Eva who is still fishing rather half-heartedly with the fork*) And what's the trouble over here, eh? Can I help – since it seems to be in fashion this evening?

Sidney takes the fork from Eva and seats her in her chair

Now. I'll give you a little tip, if you like. You'll never get a sink unblocked that way. Not by wiggling a fork about in it, like that. That's not the way to unblock a sink, now, is it? All you'll do that way, is to eventually take the chrome off your fork and possibly scratch the plug hole. Not the way. Let's see now . . . (*He runs the tap for a second and watches the water running away*) Yes. It's a little on the sluggish side. Just a little. But it'll get worse. Probably a few tea-leaves, nothing more. Let's have a look, shall we? (*He opens the cupboard under the sink*) Ten to one, this is where your troubles lie. Ah-ha. It's a good old-fashioned one, isn't it? Need the wrench for that one.

JANE   He'll soon fix that for you, won't you, Sidney?

SIDNEY   Brace of shakes. Shake of braces as we used to say in the Navy. I've got the tools. Down in the car. No trouble at all. (*He turns to Eva*) Nothing serious. All it is, you see – where the pipe bends under the sink there – they call that the trap. Now then. (*He takes out a pencil*) I'll show you. Always useful to know. Paper? (*He picks up Eva's latest suicide note*) This is nothing vital, is it . . .? Now then. (*He glances curiously at it, then turns it over and starts to draw his diagram on the back*) Now – here's your plug hole, do you see, here – if I can draw it – and this is your pipe coming straight down and then almost doubling back on itself like that, for a second, you see? Then it runs away here, to the drain . . .

JANE   You want to know anything, you ask Sidney . . .

SIDNEY   And this little bit here's the actual drain trap. And all you have to do is get it open and out it all comes. Easy when you know. Now I suppose I'll have to walk down four flights for my tools. (*He screws up the paper and throws it away. At the door*) Now, don't worry. Lottie's keeping them entertained at the moment and Dick's busy with George, so everybody's happy, aren't they?

Sidney opens the door and goes out. We hear Lottie's laughter and the dog barking distantly for a moment before the door closes

JANE   It's at times like this you're glad of your friends, aren't you? (*She goes at the oven with fresh vigour, singing cheerily*)

During the above Eva writes another brief note and places it in a prominent position on the table. She now rises and goes to a chair where there is a plastic washing basket filled with clean but unironed clothes. Coiled on top is a washing line. She returns to the table. Jane, emerging for fresh water, catches sight of her

Sorting out your laundry? You're a terror, aren't you? You're worse than me. (*She returns to her oven and resumes her song*)

Eva begins to pull the washing line from the basket. She finds one end and ties in it a crude noose. She tests the effectiveness of this on one wrist and, satisfied, pulls the rest of the rope from the basket. Every foot or so is a plastic clothes peg which she removes

I think I'm beginning to win through. I think I'm down to the metal, anyway, that's something. There's about eight layers on here.

Eva comes across a pair of knickers and two pairs of socks still pegged to the line. She removes these and replaces them in the basket

There's something stuck on the bottom here like cement. You haven't had cement for dinner lately, have you? (*She laughs*)

Eva now stands with her clothes line gazing at the ceiling. There are two light fittings and her eyes rest on the one immediately above the table. She crosses to the door, clicks a switch and just this one goes out

Whooo! Where was Moses . . .? What's happened? Bulb gone, has it? We'll get Sidney to fix that when he comes back. Keep him on the go. (*She returns to the oven again, changing her tune to something suitable like 'Dancing in the Dark'*)

Eva climbs first on to a chair then on to the table holding her rope. She removes the bulb and shade in one from the socket and places them on the table at her feet. She is beginning to yawn more and more frequently and is obviously beginning to feel the effect of the sleeping pills. Swaying slightly, she starts to tie the rope round the flex above the holder. This proves a difficult operation since she has far too much rope for the job. She finally manages a knot which loosely encircles the flex. She gives the rope a gentle tug – it holds. She tries again. It still remains in position. She gives it a third tug for luck. The rope slides down the flex as far as the bulb-holder and promptly pulls this away from the wires. The holder clatters on to the table and she is left clutching the rope. She stands swaying more pronouncedly now, a faint look of desperation on her face

Ronald enters. Behind him we hear Lottie Potter's laughter and, more distant, a dog barking

RONALD Now then, how's our little invalid getting . . . (*Seeing Eva*) Oh, good God. (*He dashes forward and steadies Eva*) My dear girl, what on earth are you doing up there?

JANE (*emerging from her oven*) Oh, no. She's a real terror, you know. (*She goes to assist Ronald in helping Eva off the table and back on to a chair*) She can't keep still for a minute. (*Reprovingly to Eva*) You could have hurt yourself up there, you silly thing.

Ronald folds up the rope, which is looped round Eva's wrist, and leaves it in her hand

RONALD Lucky I . . .

JANE Yes, it was.

RONALD I mean. What was she trying to do?

JANE Bulb's gone.

RONALD (*looking up*) Yes, so it has. Well, you could have asked me to do that, you know. I'm no handyman but even I can change a bulb.

Sidney enters with a large bag of tools. Behind him we hear Lottie's laughter and a dog barking

SIDNEY Here we are, back again. I've brought everything, just in case. Everything except the kitchen sink and that's already here, eh? (*He laughs*)

RONALD What? Oh, yes. Very good.

JANE (*amused*) Except the kitchen sink. Honestly.

SIDNEY (*noticing the light*) Hallo, hallo. More trouble? (*He puts the tool bag by the sink*)

RONALD Nothing much. Just a bulb gone.

SIDNEY You've lost more than a bulb, by the look of it. You've lost the whole fitting.

49

RONALD   Good gracious me. So we have. Look at that.

SIDNEY   Just the bare wires, you see.

RONALD   Yes. There's no thingummyjig.

JANE   Just the wires, aren't there?

SIDNEY   Don't like the look of that.

RONALD   No.

JANE   No.

SIDNEY   I mean, if that was to short across like it is . . .

RONALD   Yes.

JANE   Yes.

SIDNEY   You could finish up with a fuse, or a fire . . .

RONALD   Or worse.

JANE   Worse.

SIDNEY   I mean, you've only got to be carrying, say, for instance, a pair of aluminium steps across the room and you happen accidentally to knock against the wires, electricity would be conducted down the steps and straight into you. Natural earth, you see. Finish.

RONALD   I suppose that would go for a very tall man in, say, a tin hat, eh? (*He laughs*)

SIDNEY   True, true. Not so probable. But true.

JANE   Lucky it's not the war time.

SIDNEY   Oh, yes. In certain cases, one touch could be fatal.

RONALD   Better fix it, I suppose.

SIDNEY   I'd advise it. Going to have a go, are you?

RONALD   Well – I don't know. Looks a bit technical for me.

SIDNEY   Oh, no. Very simple. Nothing to it. Look, you've got your two wires coming down . . . Look, I'll draw it for you. (*He whips out his pencil again and, searching for a piece of paper, picks up Eva's suicide note. With a casual glance at it*) Nothing important this, is it? (*Without waiting for a reply, he turns it over and starts to sketch*)

Eva stares – fascinated

You've got your two wires coming down here, you see – like that. They go through the top of the plug, here – excuse the drawing, and then they just screw in to the little holes on the prongs, you see? Tighten your grubs. Screw your top to your bottom and away you go.

RONALD Let there be light.

SIDNEY Exactly.

Eva scrawls another note

RONALD Oh, well, that looks – simple enough. (*He still seems doubtful*)

SIDNEY Right. I'll get you a screwdriver and I'll get going on the sink. (*Opening his tool bag*) Now then, let's get you fixed up. What've we got here? (*He rummages through his tools, taking out a screwdriver and a spare fitting*)

RONALD Good gracious. What a collection.

SIDNEY This is just the set I keep in the car.

RONALD Really? Get a lot of trouble with it, do you?

During the above Eva climbs slowly on to her chair, steps on to the table and reaches out with both hands towards the bare wires. Jane, who has returned to her oven, turns in time to see her

JANE Watch her!

SIDNEY Hey-hey . . .

RONALD Hoy . . .

All three of them run, grab Eva and pull her back in the chair

SIDNEY They might have been live.

RONALD Yes. (*A thought*) Might they?

SIDNEY Yes.

RONALD Well, how do we know they're not?

SIDNEY Check the switches first.

RONALD Yes, well, don't you think we'd better? I mean, I'm going to be the one who . . .

SIDNEY (*striding to the door*) Check the switches, by all means.

Sidney plays with both switches, plunging the room into darkness a couple of times

51

JANE (*during this, still with Eva*) She's got a charmed life, honestly. The sooner that doctor gets here . . .

RONALD He'll fix her up.

JANE He'd better.

SIDNEY (*completing his check*) Yes, all safe. (*He takes off his jacket and puts it over the back of a chair*)

RONALD Ah.

SIDNEY Should be, anyway. Unless they've put this switch on upside down, of course.

RONALD How do we know they haven't?

SIDNEY Well, you'll be the first to find out, won't you? (*He roars with mirth*)

JANE (*equally tickled*) You'll be the first . . .

Ronald is less amused

SIDNEY Well, let's get down to it, shall we?

RONALD (*gazing at the light*) Yes.

SIDNEY Each to his own. (*He starts work under the sink*)

JANE Each to his own. (*She returns to the oven*)

They prepare for their various tasks

This is coming up a treat.

SIDNEY Ought to get – er – Marion out here, eh? Find her something to do.

RONALD (*clearing the things off the table*) No – no. I don't think she'd contribute very much. Probably better off with the Potters. Matter of fact, she's just a bit – on her pins. You know what I mean.

SIDNEY Ah, well. Christmas.

JANE If you can't do it at Christmas . . .

SIDNEY Once a year, eh?

RONALD Not in my wife's case. Festive season recurs rather more frequently. Every three or four days.

SIDNEY (*under the sink*) Ah-ha! You're going to be a tricky little fellow, aren't you? Nobody's opened you since you were last painted.

Sidney clatters under the sink. Jane scrubs cheerfully on. Ronald sets to work, standing on the table and on Eva's latest note. He tackles his own particular job extremely slowly and with many false starts. He is not particularly electrically-minded. Eva attempts, under the following, to rescue her note from under Ronald's feet. It rips. She scrawls another rapidly

RONALD Must be pretty pleased with your year, I should imagine.

SIDNEY Beg pardon?

RONALD Had a good year. Must be pretty pleased.

SIDNEY Oh, yes. Had a few lucky hunches. Seemed to pay off.

RONALD I should say so.

SIDNEY Mustn't complain, anyway.

JANE No. Mustn't complain.

SIDNEY As long as you're looking after our money. Eh? (*He laughs*)

RONALD Oh, yes. Yes.

They work. Sidney whistles. Ronald hums. Jane sings. Occasionally, the workers break off their respective melodies to make those sounds that people make when wrestling with inanimate objects. 'Come on, you little . . . Just one more . . . get in, get in, etc.' During this Eva, having finished her note, sees Sidney's bag of tools. Unseen by the others, she goes to the bag and removes a lethal-looking tin of paint stripper. Also a hammer and a nail. She nails her latest note to the table with the hammer which she leaves on the table. Turning her attention to the paint stripper, she tries to get the top off. It is very stiff. She struggles vainly then goes to the room door, intending to use it as a vice

At this moment Marion enters

Eva is pushed behind the door, and, as it swings shut, she clings to the handle and falls across the floor. While the door is open the dog barks and raised voices are heard

MARION (*holding a gin bottle and glass*) I say – something rather ghastly's happened.

RONALD (*concentrating hard*) Oh, yes?

MARION   Goodness! Don't you all look busy? Darling, what are you doing up there?

Eva tries to open the bottle with the walk-in cupboard door

RONALD   Oh, just a little light electrical work or should I say a little electrical light work? (*He laughs*)

SIDNEY   Electrical light work. (*He laughs*)

JANE   Electrical light work. (*She laughs*)

SIDNEY   I like that – yes . . .

MARION   Yes, very funny, darling. Now do come down, please, before you blow us all up. You know absolutely nothing about that sort of thing at all.

RONALD   I don't know . . .

MARION   Absolutely nothing.

RONALD   I fixed that bottle lamp with a cork in it, didn't I?

MARION   Yes, darling, and we all had to sit round admiring it while the lampshade burst into flames.

Eva goes to the toolbag for a screwdriver

RONALD   (*irritably*) That was entirely the fault of the bloody lampshade.

MARION   I was terrified. The whole thing was an absolute death trap. I had to give it to the Scouts for jumble.

SIDNEY   What was the trouble?

MARION   It was like modern sculpture. Bare wires sticking out at extraordinary angles.

Eva goes and sits down in a corner

SIDNEY   No. I meant when you came in.

MARION   Oh, yes. What was it? Something awful. (*She remembers*) Oh, yes. I came for help, that's right. That dog . . .

JANE   George?

MARION   Is that his name – George – yes. Well, he's just bitten that Potter man in the leg.

JANE   Oh, dear.

MARION   Terribly nasty. Right through his trousers. Of course,

54

it was entirely his fault. I mean, he was leaping about being desperately hearty with the poor animal till it had froth simply foaming from its jowls and didn't know where it was.

JANE Oh, dear, are they . . .?

SIDNEY Yes, what are they . . .?

MARION Well, I think they were thinking of going. If they haven't gone. They seem to think he might need an anti-something.

SIDNEY Rabies.

MARION Probably. I'll see. (*She opens the door*)

Silence

(*Calling*) I say, hallo. Hallo there.

There is a low growl

Oh, dear.

RONALD What's the matter?

MARION It's sort of crouching in the doorway chewing a shoe and looking terribly threatening.

RONALD Really?

MARION I don't think it's going to let us through, you know.

RONALD (*picking up the tin of dog meat and moving tentatively to the sitting room*) He's probably all right, he just needs calming down. Here, boy boy, good boy. Hallo, boy, good boy.

A growl. Ronald returns, closes the door, and goes back to his work

No, well, best to leave them when they're like that. Just a bit excited.

SIDNEY Mind you, once they've drawn blood, you know . . .

JANE Old Mr Allsop's Alsatian . . .

SIDNEY Yes.

MARION Yes. Well, it's lucky I brought the drink. Keep the workers going. And the invalid. How is she?

RONALD Very groggy.

MARION (*peering at her*) Golly, yes. She's a dreadful colour. How are you feeling?

JANE   I don't think she really knows we're here.

MARION   Hallo. Hallo, there . . . (*No response*) No, you're right. She's completely gone. Poor thing. Oh well, drink, everyone?

JANE   Not just at the moment. Nearly finished.

MARION   Jolly good. (*Nudging Sidney with her leg*) What about you?

SIDNEY   In a moment. In just a moment.

RONALD   Darling, I wouldn't drink too much more of that.

MARION   Oh, Ronnie, don't be such a misery. Honestly, he's such a misery. He's totally incapable of enjoying a party.

RONALD   No, all I'm saying is . . .

MARION   Well, Eva and I'll have one, won't we, Eva?

Marion pours out two glasses

SIDNEY   (*from under the sink*) Ah!

JANE   All right?

SIDNEY   Got it off.

JANE   Oh, well done.

MARION   What's he got off?

Eva finally gets the lid off the paint stripper and is about to drink it

SIDNEY   That was a wrestle and no mistake. But I got it off. The big question now is, can I get it on again.

MARION   Eva, dear, now you drink that. (*She puts the glass in Eva's hand, removing the tin of stripper*) That'll do you far more good than all the pills and patent medicines put together. (*She puts the paint stripper on the draining-board*)

RONALD   Marion, seriously, I wouldn't advise . . .

MARION   (*hitting him on the foot with the gin bottle*) Oh, Ronnie, just shut up!

RONALD   Ah!

MARION   (*to Eva; confidentially*) You'd never think it but he was a really vital young man, Eva. You'd never think it to look at him, would you?

Marion fills Eva's glass of gin so that she is forced in her inert state to drink some

SIDNEY (*emerging from his sink*) Well, time for a break. Now then, did somebody promise a drink?

MARION (*pushing the bottle towards him*) Help yourself.

SIDNEY Thank you.

JANE I think that's about as much as I can do. It's a bit better.

MARION (*going to the stove*) Oh, look, isn't that marvellous? Look at that splendid oven.

SIDNEY Well done. Well done.

JANE Bit of a difference. (*She picks up her bowl of water and carries it to the sink*)

RONALD (*having difficulty*) Ah . . .

SIDNEY How's the electrical department?

RONALD (*muttering*) Damn fiddly thing.

SIDNEY (*seeing Jane*) Hey! Don't pour that down now!

JANE Oh. Nearly forgot.

SIDNEY You'd have been popular. (*He puts the gin bottle on the table*)

JANE I'd have been popular.

MARION Well, I'm just going to sit here all night and admire that oven. I think she's honestly better than our Mrs Minns, isn't she, darling?

RONALD Anyone's better than our Mrs Minns.

MARION Oh, she means well. We have our Mrs Minns. She's a dear old soul. She can hardly see and she only comes in for two hours a day and when she's gone we spend the rest of the time cleaning up after her. But she's got an absolute heart of gold.

RONALD Largely paid for by us.

SIDNEY Good health. Happy Christmas to all.

MARION Happy New Year.

JANE Yes.

SIDNEY Get this lot finished, maybe there'll be time for a game . . .

JANE Oh, yes . . .

MARION What sort of game do you mean?

SIDNEY You know. Some good party game. Get everyone
jumping about.

MARION What an obscene idea.

SIDNEY Oh, they're great fun. We've had some laughs,
haven't we?

JANE Talk about laughs . . .

RONALD Blast.

SIDNEY What's the matter?

RONALD Dropped the little thing. Could you see if you can
see it. I've got to keep holding on to this or it'll drop off.
Little thing about so big.

MARION What little thing?

RONALD A whajamacallit.

JANE Small was it?

RONALD Lord, yes. Tiny little thingy.

SIDNEY Oh dear oh dear.

They hunt, Sidney crawls on hands and knees

JANE Might have rolled anywhere.

MARION What are we looking for?

RONALD Little whosit. Goes in here.

MARION Darling, do be more precise. What's a whosit?

JANE You know, one of those – one of those – isn't that silly,
I can't think of the word.

MARION Well, I refuse to look till I know what we're looking
for. We could be here all night. I mean, from the look of this
floor it's simply littered with little whosits.

SIDNEY (*under the table*) Can't see it.

JANE It's on the tip of my tongue . . . that's it, a nut. Little
nut.

MARION (*searching by the sink*) Oh, well then, a nut. Now we
know. Everyone hunt for a little nut.

Eva goes and sits at the table

SIDNEY I didn't know we were looking for a nut.

JANE Aren't we?

RONALD   No. A screw. That's what I'm after, a screw.

SIDNEY   A screw, yes.

JANE   Oh, a screw.

MARION   All right, everybody, stop looking for nuts. Ronnie's now decided he wants a screw. I can't see a thing, and I think it would be terribly sensible if we put the light on, wouldn't it?

RONALD   Good idea.

Marion goes to the light switch.

SIDNEY   (*realizing far too late*) No, I wouldn't turn that on . . .

Marion presses the switch

MARION   There.

Ronald, on the table, starts vibrating, emitting a low moan

SIDNEY   (*rising*) Turn it off.

JANE   Get him away.

MARION   Darling, what on earth are you doing?

JANE   (*reaching out to pull Ronald away*) Get him away.

SIDNEY   No, don't touch him, he's live. (*He goes to the switch*)

Jane touches him and recoils, with a squeak

RONALD   (*through gritted teeth*) Somebody turn it off.

Sidney turns it off

SIDNEY   All right. Panic over.

Ronald continues to vibrate

JANE   Turn him off, Sidney.

SIDNEY   I have.

JANE   Turn him off!

SIDNEY   He is off. (*Calming Jane*) Now, pull yourself together. Help me get him down. Get him down.

Sidney and Jane guide Ronald down from the table and guide him to a chair. Marion watches them

MARION   Good Lord. Wasn't that extraordinary?

SIDNEY   Easy now.

JANE   Take it slowly.

Eva pours herself another drink

MARION   Whenever he fiddles about with anything electrical it always ends in disaster. This always happens. Is he all right?

SIDNEY   He's in a state of shock.

JANE   He would be.

SIDNEY   Sit him down and keep him warm – that's the way. Pass me my jacket. Jacket. Jacket.

MARION   He looks frightfully odd.

JANE   (*bringing Sidney's jacket*) Here.

SIDNEY   He needs more. He really needs to be wrapped up, otherwise . . .

JANE   (*looking round*) There's nothing much here.

SIDNEY   Well, find something. In the other room. We need blankets.

JANE   Right.

Jane goes to the door whilst Marion looks vaguely round the kitchen

SIDNEY   Now easy, old chap. Just keep breathing . . .

Jane opens the door. There is a fierce growling. She withdraws swiftly and closes it

JANE   He's still there.

SIDNEY   Who?

JANE   The dog.

SIDNEY   Well, step over him. This is an emergency.

JANE   I'm not stepping over him. You step over him.

SIDNEY   Oh dear oh dear.

MARION   (*who has found the washing basket*) What about these bits and bobs? (*She picks up an article of clothing*)

SIDNEY   What's that?

MARION   Last week's washing, I think. (*Sniffing it*) It seems fairly clean. Might be better than nothing.

SIDNEY   Yes, well, better than nothing.

MARION   It seems dry.

JANE   Better than nothing.

Between them, during the following, they cover Ronald in an assortment of laundry, both male and female. He finishes up more or less encased in it but still quivering

SIDNEY   Quick as you can. Come along, quick as you can.

JANE   (*examining a shirt*) She hasn't got this collar very clean.

SIDNEY   Jane, come along.

MARION   (*holding up a petticoat*) Oh, that's rather pretty. I wonder where she got this.

SIDNEY   Not the time for that now. That the lot?

MARION   Yes. Only socks left. And you-know-whats.

SIDNEY   Well, it'll keep his temperature up.

MARION   Oh, my God, what does he look like? Ronnie! You know I've got a terrible temptation to phone up his chief cashier. If he could see him now . . . (*She starts to laugh*)

JANE   I don't think he's very well, you know.

MARION   Yes, I'm sorry. It's just that I've never seen anything quite so ludicrous.

SIDNEY   (*moving a stool up beside Ronald*) Might I suggest that Marion sits down with her husband just until the doctor gets here for Mrs Jackson . . .

JANE   Then he can look at them both.

SIDNEY   Precisely.

JANE   Lucky he was coming.

SIDNEY   Yes, well, we'd better just finish off and clear up, hadn't we?

MARION   (*sitting beside Ronald*) Would you like a drink, darling? You look dreadful!

61

JANE   I'd better just go over the floor.

SIDNEY   (*preparing to go under the sink again*) No, dear, we don't want you to go over the floor. Not now . . .

JANE   Just where we've been tramping about. If Doctor's coming. It won't take a minute.

SIDNEY   All right. Carry on, Sister. Sorry I spoke.

JANE   (*going to the walk-in cupboard*) Now where does she keep her broom?

RONALD   (*strained tone*) You know, I feel very peculiar.

Jane finds the broom and starts clearing the immediate vicinity around the table

MARION   Well, I hope you won't be like this all over Christmas, darling. I mean we've got your mother over tomorrow for lunch and Edith and the twins on Boxing Day – I just couldn't face them alone, I just couldn't.

JANE   (*to Eva*) Excuse me, dear. I wonder if you could just . . . (*She winds up the rope, still looped to Eva's wrist, and puts it in Eva's hand*) Tell you what, why don't you sit up here? Just for a second. Then I won't get in the way of your feet. (*She assists Eva to sit on the edge of the table*) Upsidaisy.

SIDNEY   (*sliding under the sink*) She all right still?

JANE   I think so.

Eva yawns

Just a bit tired. Neglected you in all the excitement, haven't we? Never mind. Just sit there. Doctor'll be here soon. (*She sweeps under the table*)

MARION   You know, I believe I'm beginning to feel dizzy as well. I hope I haven't caught it from her.

JANE   I hope not. What a Christmas, eh?

SIDNEY   (*from under the sink*) We'll be laughing about this.

JANE   (*going to the sink and lifting Sidney's feet*) Excuse me, dear. What's that?

SIDNEY   I say, in about two weeks' time, we'll –

Jane pours the water away in the sink

    – all be sitting down and laughing about – aaaah!

JANE Oh, no.

SIDNEY Put the plug in.

JANE (*feverishly following the plug chain*) I can't find the end.

SIDNEY Put the plug in!

JANE (*putting the plug in*) I'm sorry.

SIDNEY (*emerging from under the sink, his top half drenched in dirty water*) Look what you've done.

JANE I'm terribly sorry. (*She picks up a dish cloth*)

SIDNEY Look what you have done! You silly woman!

She tries to mop him down with the dish cloth

    (*Beating her away*) Don't do that! Don't do that! It's too late for that. Look at this shirt. This is a new shirt.

JANE Well, it'll wash. It'll wash. I'll wash it. It's only oven grease.

SIDNEY I told you, didn't I? I said, whatever you do–don't pour water down there, didn't I?

JANE I didn't think . . .

SIDNEY Obviously.

JANE Well, take the shirt off now and I'll . . .

SIDNEY And I'll go home in my singlet, I suppose?

JANE Nobody'll notice.

SIDNEY Of course they'll notice. Otherwise, there'd be no point in wearing a shirt in the first place, would there? If nobody noticed, we'd all be walking around in our singlets.

JANE It's dark.

SIDNEY Don't change the subject. It would really teach you a lesson if I caught pneumonia.

JANE (*tearful*) Don't say that.

SIDNEY Teach you, that would.

Jane sniffs. Sidney strides to the door

    Dear oh dear.

63

JANE (*following him*) Where are you going?

SIDNEY To get my overcoat before I freeze. Where else do you think I'm going?

JANE But, Sidney . . .

Sidney ignores her, flinging open the door and striding out, making a dignified exit. There is a burst of furious barking. Sidney reappears very swiftly and closes the door behind him

SIDNEY (*to Eva; furiously*) That dog of yours is a liability. You ought to keep that animal under control. I can't even get to my overcoat. It's not good enough.

Eva slowly lies down on the kitchen table, oblivious

JANE Come and sit down.

SIDNEY Sit down? What's the point of sitting down?

JANE Geoff should be back soon.

SIDNEY I should hope so. This isn't what you expect at all. Not when you come round for a quiet drink and a chat. (*Almost screaming in Eva's ear*) This is the last time I accept hospitality in this household.

JANE Ssh.

SIDNEY What?

JANE She'll hear you.

SIDNEY I don't care who hears me. (*He sits*)

JANE Ssh. (*She sits*)

A pause. The four of them are sitting. Eva lies. Ronald continues to look glassy, quivering slightly; Marion's drinking has caught up with her. Jane looks abjectly miserable. Sidney shivers in his vest.

SIDNEY And we're missing the television.

JANE Ssh.

A silence. Then, from apparently nowhere, a sleepy voice begins to sing dreamily. It is Eva

EVA (*singing*) 'On the first day of Christmas my true love sent to me, a partridge in a pear tree. On the second

day of Christmas my true love sent to me, two turtle
doves –

MARION (*joining her*) – and a partridge in a pear tree. On the
third day of Christmas my true love sent to me, three French
hens –

JANE (*joining her*) – two turtle doves and a partridge in a pear
tree. On the fourth day of Christmas my true love sent to
me, four calling birds –

RONALD (*joining them*) – three French hens, two turtle doves
and a partridge in a pear tree.

ALL On the fifth day of Christmas my true love sent to me, five
gold rings, etc.

*As the bedraggled quintet begin to open up, the singing gets bolder and
more confident. Somewhere in the distance George begins to howl. Eva,
still lying on her back, conducts them dreamily with both hands and then
finally with the hammer*

The door bursts open. Geoffrey enters hurriedly, calling behind him

GEOFFREY Through here, Doctor. Please hurry, I . . .

*Geoffrey is suddenly aware of the sound behind him. He turns, still
breathless from his run up four flights. His mouth drops further open
as he surveys the scene. The singing continues unabated, as the Lights
black-out and –*

the CURTAIN *falls*

Act Three

The Brewster-Wrights' kitchen. Next Christmas

They live in a big old Victorian house, and the kitchen, though modernized to some extent, still retains a lot of the flavour of the original room. A sink, an electric stove (or even an Aga range), a fridge, a dark wood sideboard, a round table and chairs form the substantial furnishings for the room. On the table is an elderly radio set. There is a door, half of opaque glass, to the hall, and a garden door

When the CURTAIN *rises, Ronald is discovered sitting in an armchair near the table. He wears a scarf and a green eye-shade. Beside him is a lighted portable oil stove. At his elbow is an empty teacup. The radio is on, playing very quietly a very jolly carol. Ronald is reading a book. He is obviously enjoying it, for every two or three seconds he chuckles to himself out loud. This continues for some seconds, until the door from the hall opens and Eva enters. She wears a winter coat and carries an empty teacup and plate, which she puts down on the draining-board*

RONALD   Oh. Hallo there.

EVA   All right?

RONALD   Oh, yes. (*He switches off the radio*)

EVA   Are you warm enough in here?

RONALD   Oh, yes. It's fine in here. Well, not too bad.

EVA   The rest of the house is freezing. I don't envy you going to bed.

RONALD   Her room's all right, though, is it?

EVA   Oh, she's got three electric fires blazing away.

RONALD   My God. That'll be the second power station I've paid for this winter.

EVA   She seems to be rather dug in up there. Almost in a state of hibernation. Doesn't she ever come out?

RONALD   Not if she can help it. Heating system went on the blink, you see – usual thing and we had a few frosty words

66

over it and – the outcome was, she said she wasn't setting foot outside her room until I got it fixed.

EVA (*putting on a pair of gloves*) Well, how long's it been like this?

RONALD (*vaguely*) Oh, I don't know. Two or three weeks, I suppose.

EVA Well, that's disgusting. Can't you get the men round to fix it?

RONALD Yes, yes. I have phoned them several times. But I've been a bit unlucky up to now. They always seem to be at lunch . . .

EVA (*taking off her coat and putting it on the back of a chair*) Well, I wouldn't put up with it. I'd scream the place down till Geoffrey got it fixed. (*She hunts in the cupboards*)

RONALD Yes, we've had a packet of trouble with this central heating. Always goes on the blink. Either the day before Christmas, the day before Easter or the day before Whitsun. Always seems to manage it. Don't understand the principle it works on but whatever it is, seems to be very closely tied in with the Church calendar. (*He laughs*) Can I help you at all?

EVA She said she'd like a sandwich. (*She puts a plate, knife, bread and a pot of peanut butter on a bread board*)

RONALD (*looking at his watch*) Oh, yes. She's about due for a sandwich.

EVA I'm looking for the butter.

RONALD Oh. don't you bother to do that, I'll . . .

EVA It's all right. Where do you keep your butter?

RONALD Do you know, that's very interesting. I have absolutely no idea. A closely guarded secret kept by Mrs Minns. I suppose we could hazard a guess. Now then, butter. Try the fridge.

EVA Fridge?

RONALD Keeps it soft. It's warmer in there than it is outside.

EVA (*looking in the fridge*) Right first time. (*She sets about making a sandwich, taking off one glove*)

67

RONALD What's she want? Peanut butter?

EVA Apparently.

RONALD Good grief. She's got an absolute craving for that stuff lately. That and cheese footballs. All most alarming. She's not up there knitting little blue bootees, by any chance?

EVA Not that I noticed.

RONALD Thank God for that.

EVA She looks a lot better than when I last saw her, anyway.

RONALD Really? Yes, yes. Well, she got a bit overtired, I think. Principally.

EVA Geoff'll be here in a minute to pick me up. I'll get out of your way. I just heard Marion was – I hope you didn't mind . . .

RONALD No, very good of you to look round. Sure she appreciated it. She doesn't get many visitors. Lottie Potter looked in briefly. That set her back a couple of weeks. No, the trouble with Marion you see, is she lives on her nerves. Far too much.

EVA Marion does?

RONALD Oh, yes. Very nervous, insecure sort of person basically, you know.

EVA Really?

RONALD That surprises you, does it? Well, I've got a pretty thorough working knowledge of her now, you know. I mean, she's calmer than she was. When I first met her she was really one of the jumpiest girls you could ever hope to meet. Still, as I say, she's much calmer since she's been with me. If I've done nothing else for her, I've acted as a sort of sedative.

EVA You don't think that a lot of her trouble may be – drink?

RONALD Drink? No, I don't honestly think so. She's always liked a – I mean, the doctor did say she should lay off. But that was only because it was acting as a stimulant. She hasn't touched it lately.

EVA She has this evening.

RONALD Really?

EVA Yes.

RONALD Well, you do surprise me.

EVA She's got quite a collection up there.

RONALD Oh, has she? Has she now?

EVA Didn't you know?

RONALD Well, I don't often have much cause to go into her room these days. She likes her privacy, you see. And I respect that. Not that it's not a mutual arrangement, you understand. I mean, she doesn't particularly choose to come into my room either. So it works out rather conveniently. On the whole.

EVA Do you ever see each other at all?

RONALD Good Lord, it's not as if we aren't in the same house. We bang into each other quite frequently. It's not always as quiet as this, believe me. In the holidays we've got the boys here. They thump about. No end of a racket. Boys, of course. Mind you, they're no trouble –they're usually out, too, most of the time – with their friends.

EVA Pity they're not with you for Christmas.

RONALD Oh well, it's greatly over-estimated, this Christmas business. That reminds me, would you like a drink? Seeing as it's Christmas.

EVA No, I don't think so.

RONALD Oh, go on. Just one. With me, for Christmas.

EVA Well – all right, a little one.

RONALD Right. (*He rises*) Good. I'll brave the elements then and try and make it as far as the sitting-room . . .

The doorbell rings

EVA That's probably Geoff.

RONALD (*opening the door*) I'll let him in, then. (*Stopping short*) Good Lord, is that dust on the hall table or frost? Won't be a minute.

Ronald goes out

69

Eva, alone, looks round the room rather sadly. She leaves the sandwich and plate on the table, puts the other things back on the sideboard, returns to the table, sits and starts to eat the sandwich

Geoffrey enters in his overcoat

GEOFFREY   Blimey. Why aren't you sitting in the garden, it's warmer.

EVA   Hullo.

GEOFFREY   Ready then?

EVA   I'm just going to have a drink with Ronnie.

GEOFFREY   Oh. And how is *she*?

EVA   Drunk.

GEOFFREY   God.

Pause. Eva munches

EVA   How did you get on?

GEOFFREY   Well . . .

EVA   Did you ask him?

GEOFFREY   Well . . .

EVA   You didn't.

Geoffrey does not reply

You didn't damn well ask him.

GEOFFREY   It's no good. I find it impossible to ask people for money.

Eva gives a short laugh

I'm sorry.

EVA   He owes it you. You're not asking him a favour, you know. He owes it you.

GEOFFREY   I know.

EVA   Well then.

GEOFFREY   It doesn't matter.

EVA   Oh, my . . . Oh well, I'll have to get in touch with him then. After Christmas. I don't mind doing it.

GEOFFREY   You don't have to do that.

EVA   Well, somebody has to, darling. Don't they?

The door opens. A drinks trolley enters followed by Ronald

RONALD   Here we come. The Trans-Siberian Express. Thank you so much. We seem to be a bit depleted on the old alcohol stakes. Odd, thought I'd stocked up only recently. Probably old Mrs Minns been knocking them off, eh? The woman must have some vices. She hasn't got much else to recommend her. Now what are we having? Eva?

EVA   Could I have just a bitter lemon?

RONALD   Good gracious, nothing stronger?

EVA   Not just now.

RONALD   Well, if that's what you want . . . Geoff, what about you?

GEOFFREY   I think I'd like the same, actually.

RONALD   What? A bitter lemon?

GEOFFREY   Just what I feel like.

RONALD   You won't last through Christmas at that rate. (*Inspecting his trolley*) Well, that seems to be the only thing I haven't brought.

EVA   Oh well, it doesn't matter. Something else.

RONALD   No, no. I'll get it, I'll get it. We've got some somewhere.

Ronald goes out, closing the door

EVA   I mean, either you want me to help you or you don't.

GEOFFREY   Yes.

EVA   I mean, if you don't, just say so. I don't particularly enjoy working in that dark little office of yours. You're a terrible employer. You come in late even when I drive you to work. You take four-hour lunch breaks and then expect me to do all your damn typing at five o'clock in the evening.

GEOFFREY   That's the way I do business.

EVA   Not with me you don't.

GEOFFREY   That's what you're paid for.

EVA   That's what I'm what?

71

GEOFFREY Look, if you don't like the job . . .

EVA You asked me to help you. Now, if you didn't mean that, that's a different matter.

GEOFFREY Well yes, I did, but . . .

EVA All right, then. That's settled. You asked me to help you. I am bloody well going to help you.

GEOFFREY O.K. O.K., thanks.

EVA Not at all. (*A slight pause*) And you're not going to ask for the money?

GEOFFREY No.

EVA Even though we're owed it?

GEOFFREY No.

EVA And you won't let me ask?

GEOFFREY No.

EVA All right. Then we'll have to think of something else.

GEOFFREY Exactly.

EVA I'll phone Sidney Hopcroft after Christmas and talk to him.

GEOFFREY Sidney Hopcroft.

EVA He's always asking if you're interested.

GEOFFREY If you think I'm going to get myself involved in his seedy little schemes . . .

EVA Why not?

GEOFFREY Have you seen the buildings he's putting up? Half his tenants are asking to be re-housed and they haven't even moved in yet.

EVA Darling, I hate to remind you but ever since the ceiling of the Harrison building caved in and nearly killed the manager, Sidney Hopcroft is about your only hope of surviving as an architect in this city.

GEOFFREY I can do without Sidney Hopcroft, thank you very much.

The door opens. Ronald enters with two bottles of bitter lemon

RONALD Here we are. Two very bitter lemons. (*He pours out two bitter lemons and a Scotch*)

EVA Thank you.

RONALD I think I'm going to have something more than that, if you'll excuse me. Bit quieter than last Christmas, eh?

GEOFFREY What?

RONALD Last Christmas. Remember that? Round at your place?

GEOFFREY Yes.

EVA Yes.

RONALD Good gracious me. You have to laugh now. Old Hopcroft. (*He laughs*) Always remember old Hopcroft. Doing very well. Did you know that? Doing frightfully well. Seems to have a flair for it. Wouldn't think so to look at him. Always found him a bit unprepossessing. Still – the chap to keep in with. The rate he's going.

EVA Yes.

GEOFFREY (*picking up Ronald's book*) Is this good?

RONALD Oh, yes. Yes, quite good. Very amusing. Bit – saucy, in parts. Mrs Minns found it under one of the boys' mattresses. Nearly finished her there and then, poor old thing. Bitter lemon.

EVA Thanks.

RONALD Bitter lemon.

GEOFFREY Thank you.

RONALD (*raising his glass of Scotch*) Well, Happy Christmas. Good health. God bless.

EVA Happy Christmas.

GEOFFREY Happy Christmas.

RONALD (*after a pause*) Sorry to hear about your problems, Geoff.

GEOFFREY How do you mean?

RONALD I meant, the Harrison thing. Hear it fell through . . . Oh, I'm sorry, perhaps that's the wrong expression to use – bit unfortunate.

GEOFFREY That's all right.

EVA It wasn't actually Geoff's fault.

RONALD No, no, I'm sure – knowing Geoff. Unthinkable. I

73

mean, that local paper's as biased as hell. I refused to read that particular article. So did all my friends.

EVA *(after a pause)* Just because Geoffrey was doing something totally new for a change . . .

GEOFFREY How's the bank doing, then?

RONALD Oh, well. We're not in the red, yet. No thanks to me, mind you.

A bell rings

GEOFFREY Is that the front door?

RONALD No. It's the – er – bedroom bell, actually. We've never bothered to have them taken out. They always come in useful. Boys with measles and so on.

EVA Shall I go up to her?

RONALD No, no, I'll . . .

EVA No, it's all right. I don't mind . . .

RONALD Well, that's very good of you. Probably nothing important. Wants the page of her magazine turning over or something.

EVA I hope not.

RONALD What's the harm, I say. As long as it keeps her happy.

EVA Yes.

Eva goes out, closing the door

RONALD I mean, who are we to argue with a woman, eh? You can never win. Hopeless. Mind you, I'm talking to the wrong chap, aren't I?

GEOFFREY What?

RONALD I mean you seem to do better than most of us.

GEOFFREY Oh, yes. *(He sits in the armchair)*

RONALD You seem to have got things pretty well organized on the home front. *(He laughs)*

GEOFFREY Well, it's just a matter of knowing . . .

RONALD Ah yes, that's the point. I never really have. Not really. I mean, take my first wife. Distinguished-looking woman. Very charming. Seemed pretty happy on the whole. Then one day, she suddenly ups and offs and goes. Quite amazing. I mean, I had literally no idea she was going to. I mean, we had the flat over the bank at the time, so it wasn't as if I was even very far away and on this particular day, I came up for lunch and she'd laid on her usual splendid meal. I mean I had absolutely no complaints about that. I think my very words were something like, jolly nice that, see you this evening. And when we knocked off for tea, I came upstairs and she'd just taken off. Well, I hunted about for a bit in case she'd got knocked down or gone shopping and lost her memory or something and then she wrote, some time later, and said she'd had enough. So I was forced to call it a day. Some time later again, I took up tennis to forget her and married Marion. Of course, that's all forgotten now. All the same, sometimes in the evening I can't help sitting here and trying to work it all out. I mean, something happened. Something must have happened. I'm just not sure what. Anyway. Under the bridge, eh? All I'm saying really, is some people seem to have the hang of it and some of us just aren't so lucky.

GEOFFREY Hang of what?

RONALD Well – this whole women business, really. I mean, this may sound ridiculous, but I've never to this day really known what most women think about anything. Completely closed book to me. I mean, God bless them, what would we do without them? But I've never understood them. I mean, damn it all, one minute you're having a perfectly good time and the next, you suddenly see them there like – some old sports jacket or something – literally beginning to come apart at the seams. Floods of tears, smashing your pots, banging the furniture about. God knows what. Both my wives, God bless them, they've given me a great deal of pleasure over the years but, by God, they've cost me a fortune in fixtures and fittings. All the same. Couldn't do without them, could we? I suppose. Want another one of those?

GEOFFREY No, thanks.

The door opens. Eva enters

Geoffrey rises and sits again

EVA (*coming in swiftly and closing the door*) Brrr.

RONALD Ah.

EVA Forgot to put my coat on. (*She puts her coat on*)

RONALD Anything serious?

EVA No. (*Kneeling by the stove to warm herself*) She says she wants to come down.

RONALD Here? Is that wise?

EVA She says she wants a Christmas drink with us since we're all here.

RONALD Oh well. Sort of thing she does. Calls you all the way upstairs to tell you she's coming all the way downstairs. Your drink there.

EVA Thanks.

RONALD And how's that mad dog of yours? Still chewing up your guests?

GEOFFREY Er – no . . .

EVA No, we had to – give him away.

RONALD No, really?

EVA Yes – he got a bit much. He was really getting so expensive to keep. And then these people we know who've got a farm – they said they'd have him.

RONALD Oh, dear. I didn't know that. That's a shame.

EVA Yes, it was an awful decision to make. We just felt – well . . .

GEOFFREY You did, you mean.

EVA Darling, we couldn't afford to keep him.

RONALD Well, old Dick Potter will be relieved, anyway. What did he have to have? Three stitches or something, wasn't it?

EVA Something like that.

RONALD Doesn't seem to have done him any harm, anyway. He should be half-way up some Swiss mountain by now. Hopefully, those two lads of ours are safely roped to him.

EVA   Oh, is that where they've gone?

RONALD   Yes. Something I always meant to take them on myself. Anyway, we'll have to do without old Dick to jolly us up this year. I suppose.

GEOFFREY   That's a pity.

The door opens. Marion sweeps in. She wears a negligée. She stands dramatically and flings out her arms

MARION   Geoff, darling, it's sweet of you and Eva to come round and see me.

GEOFFREY   (*rising*) Oh, that's O.K.

MARION   No, you don't know how much it means to me. It really is terribly, terribly sweet of you.

GEOFFREY   That's all right, we were . . .

MARION   And at Christmas, particularly. Bless you for remembering Christmas. (*She collapses into the armchair*)

RONALD   Look, Marion, you're going to freeze to death. For goodness' sake, put something on, woman.

MARION   I'm all right.

RONALD   Let me get you your coat. You've only just got out of bed.

MARION   Darling, I am quite all right. And I am not sitting in my kitchen in a coat. Nobody sits in a kitchen in a coat. Except tradesmen. It's unheard of. Now, offer me a drink.

RONALD   Look, dear, you know the doctor said very plainly . . .

MARION   (*snapping fiercely*) Oh, for the love of God, Ronnie, it's Christmas. Don't be such an utter misery. (*To the others*) He's Scrooge, you know. He's Scrooge in person. Have you noticed, he's turned all the heating off.

Ronald, dignified, goes to the trolley and pours Marion a drink. Geoffrey sits by the table

Oh, it's heavenly to be up. When you've lain in bed for any length of time, on your own, no-one to talk to, with just your thoughts, don't you find your whole world just begins to

77

crowd in on you? Till it becomes almost unbearable. You just lie there thinking, oh God, it could've been so much better if only I'd had the sense to do so and so – you finish up lying there utterly filled with self-loathing.

EVA   I know the feeling.

RONALD   (*handing Marion a glass*) Here you are, dear.

MARION   Heavens! I can hardly see it. Is there anything in here? No it's all right. I'll just sit here and inhale it. (*Turning to Geoffrey and Eva*) How are you, anyway?

EVA   Well, as I told you we're – pretty well . . .

MARION   I don't know what it is about Christmas but – I know it's supposed to be a festive thing and we're all supposed to be enjoying ourselves – I just find myself remembering all the dreadful things – the dreadful things I've said – the dreadful things I've done and all those awful hurtful things I didn't mean – oh God, I didn't mean them. Forgive me, I didn't mean them. (*She starts to cry*)

RONALD   Look, darling, do try and jolly up just for a bit, for heaven's sake.

MARION   (*savagely*) Jolly up? How the hell can – I – jolly – up?

EVA   Marion, dear . . .

MARION   Do you know what I saw in the hall just now? In the mirror. My face. My God, I saw my face. It was like seeing my face for the first time.

RONALD   Oh, come on. It's not a bad face, old sausage.

MARION   How could anything be so cruel? How could anything be so unutterably cruel?

RONALD   (*to Geoffrey*) Now, you see, this is a case in point. What am I supposed to do? I mean, something I've said has obviously upset her, but you tell me – you tell me.

MARION   (*pulling Geoffrey to her*) Geoff – Geoff – Geoff – did you know, Geoff, I used to be a very beautiful woman? I was a very, very beautiful woman. People used to stare at me in the street and say, 'My God, what a beautiful, beautiful woman she is.' People used to come from miles and miles just to take my picture . . .

RONALD Marion.

MARION I mean, who'd want my photograph now? Do you want my photograph now? No, of course you don't. Nobody wants my photograph now. Can anybody think of anyone who'd want a photograph of me now? Please, someone. Someone, please want my photograph.

RONALD (*bellowing*) *Marion!* Nobody wants your damn picture, now shut up.

A silence. Geoffrey and Eva are stunned. Ronald removes his eyeshade and adjusts his scarf

(*The first to recover*) Now then, what were we saying?

The doorbell rings

EVA (*after a pause*) Doorbell.

RONALD Bit late for a doorbell, isn't it?

They sit. The doorbell rings again

EVA Shall I see who it is?

RONALD Yes, do. Have a look through the little glass window. If you don't like the look of them, don't open the door.

EVA Right.

Eva goes into the hall

RONALD Can't think who'd be ringing doorbells at this time of night.

GEOFFREY Carol singers?

RONALD Not at this time. Anyway, we don't get many of them. Marion always asks them in. Insists on filling them up with hot soup and chocolate biscuits as if they were all starving. Had a great row with the chap next door. She made his children as sick as pigs.

Eva enters. As she does so the doorbell rings. She closes the door behind her

79

EVA   I couldn't be sure but it looks suspiciously like the Hopcrofts. Do you want them in?

RONALD   Oh, good grief, hardly.

GEOFFREY   Heaven forbid.

RONALD   If we sit quiet, they'll go away.

EVA   Well, there's the hall light.

RONALD   That doesn't mean anything. People always leave their hall lights on for burglars. I don't know why they bother. I mean, there must be very few households who actually choose to spend their evenings sitting in the hall with the rest of the house in the darkness.

GEOFFREY   If I know the Hopcrofts, they won't give up easily. They'll come round the side.

MARION   Why don't you just go in the hall and shout 'Go away' through the letter-box?

RONALD   Because he happens to have a very large deposit account with my bank.

The doorbell rings

EVA   They can smell us.

RONALD   I think we'll compromise and turn off the lights in here. Just to be on the safe side. (*Going to the door*) Everybody sit down and sit tight. (*By the switch*) Ready? Here we go.

The room plunges into darkness. Just two streams of light – one from the door and one from the window

Now if we all keep absolutely quiet, there's no chance of them – ow! (*He cannons into Eva who gives a cry*) I'm terribly sorry. I do beg your pardon. Was that your . . .?

EVA   That's all right.

GEOFFREY   Ssh.

RONALD   I wish I knew where I was.

GEOFFREY   Well, stand still. I think someone's coming round the side.

EVA   Ssh.

Marion starts to giggle

RONALD Marion. Quiet.

MARION I'm sorry, I've just seen the funny side . . .

GEOFFREY Ssh.

Sidney and Jane appear at the back door. They wear party hats, are decked with the odd streamer, have had more drinks than they are used to and have a carrier bag full of goodies. They both press their faces against the back door, straining to see in

MARION It's them.

GEOFFREY Ssh.

Pause

RONALD I say . . .

EVA What?

RONALD I've got a nasty feeling I didn't lock the back door.

MARION Oh, no . . .

Geoffrey and Eva hide in front of the table. Ronald steps up into a corner by the window. The back door opens slowly

SIDNEY Hallo?

JANE (*unwilling to enter*) Sidney . . .

SIDNEY Come on.

JANE But there's nobody . . .

SIDNEY The door was open, wasn't it? Of course there's some-body. They're probably upstairs.

JANE But, Sidney, they might . . .

SIDNEY Look, would you kindly not argue with me any more tonight, Jane. I haven't yet forgiven you for that business at the party. How did you manage to drop a whole plate of trifle?

JANE I didn't clean it up, Sidney, I didn't clean it up.

SIDNEY No. You just stood there with the mess at your feet. For all the world to see.

JANE Well, what . . .

81

SIDNEY   I have told you before. If you drop something like that at a stand-up party, you move away and keep moving. Now come along.

JANE   I can't see.

SIDNEY   Then wait there and I'll find the light.

A pause. Sidney crosses the room. Geoffrey and Eva creep to the side-board. The light goes on. Sidney and Jane are by the separate doors. The other four are in various absurd frozen postures obviously caught in the act of trying to find a hiding-place. Jane gives a short squeak of alarm. A long pause

MARION   (*eventually*) Boo.

SIDNEY   Good gracious.

RONALD   (*as if seeing them for the first time*) Ah, hallo there. It's you.

SIDNEY   Well, you had us fooled. They had us fooled there, didn't they?

JANE   Yes, they had us fooled.

SIDNEY   Playing a game on us, weren't you?

ALL   Yes.

EVA   Yes, we were playing a game.

SIDNEY   Completely fooled. Walked straight into that. Well, Happy Christmas, all.

ALL   (*lamely, variously*) Happy Christmas.

SIDNEY   (*after a pause*) Well.

JANE   Well.

A pause

RONALD   Would you like a drink? Now you're here.

SIDNEY   Oh, thank you.

JANE   Thank you very much.

SIDNEY   Since we're here.

RONALD   Well. What'll it be? (*He goes to the trolley*)

SIDNEY   Sherry, please.

JANE   Yes, a sherry.

SIDNEY   Yes. We'd better stick to sherry.

RONALD Sherry . . . (*He starts to pour*)

SIDNEY Sorry if we surprised you.

MARION Quite all right.

SIDNEY We knew you were here.

RONALD How?

SIDNEY We saw the car.

JANE Saw your car.

RONALD Oh. Yes.

A pause. Sidney blows a party 'blower'

EVA Been to a party?

SIDNEY Yes.

JANE Yes.

GEOFFREY You look as if you have.

SIDNEY Yes. Up at Walter's place. Walter Harrison.

RONALD Oh – old Harrison's.

SIDNEY Oh of course, you'll know him, won't you?

RONALD Oh, yes.

GEOFFREY Yes.

SIDNEY (*to Geoffrey*) Oh, yes of course. Asking you if you know old Harrison. I should think you do know old Harrison. He certainly remembers you. In fact he was saying this evening . . .

RONALD Two sherries.

SIDNEY Oh, thank you.

JANE Thank you very much.

SIDNEY Compliments of the season.

JANE Of the season.

RONALD Yes. Indeed.

A pause

SIDNEY What a house. Beautiful.

MARION Oh, do you like it? Thank you.

SIDNEY No. Old Harrison's. What a place.

JANE Lovely.

RONALD Didn't know you knew him.

SIDNEY   Well, I won't pretend. The reason we went was half
   pleasure and half – well, 'nuff said. Follow me? You scratch
   my back, I'll scratch yours.
RONALD   Ah.

A pause

JANE   It's a nice kitchen . . .
MARION   At the Harrisons'?
JANE   No. Here.
MARION   Oh. Glad you approve.

A pause

JANE   (*very, very quietly*) Sidney.
SIDNEY   Eh?
JANE   (*mouthing and gesticulating towards the carrier bag*) Their
   presents.
SIDNEY   What's that? (*He looks at his flies*)
JANE   (*still mouthing and miming*) Shall we give them their
   presents now?
SIDNEY   Yes, yes, of course. That's why we've brought them.
JANE   We brought you a present.
SIDNEY   Just a little seasonal something.
RONALD   Oh.
MARION   Ah.
EVA   Thank you.
JANE   (*to Eva*) No, I'm afraid we didn't bring you and your
   husband anything. We didn't know you'd be here, you see.
SIDNEY   Sorry about that.
EVA   Oh, never mind.
GEOFFREY   Not to worry.
JANE   We could give them the hm-mm. You know that we got
   given this evening.
SIDNEY   The what?
JANE   You know, the hm-mm. That we got in the thing.
SIDNEY   What, that? They don't want that.
JANE   No, I meant for hm-mm, you know. Hm-mm.

SIDNEY Well, if you want to. Now, come on. Give Ron and Marion their presents. They're dying to open them.

RONALD Rather.

MARION Thrilling.

JANE (*delving into her carrier and consulting the labels on various parcels*) Now this is for Ron. (*Reading*) To Ron with love from Sidney and Jane.

SIDNEY (*handing Ronald the present*) That's for you.

RONALD Thank you. (*He unwraps it*)

JANE Now then, what's this?

SIDNEY Is that Marion's?

JANE No, that's from you and me to Auntie Gloria. (*Rummaging again*) Here we are. To Marion with love from Sidney and Jane.

SIDNEY This is for you. (*He gives Marion her present*)

MARION Oh, super . . . (*To Ronald*) What've you got, darling?

RONALD (*gazing at his present mystified*) Oh, yes. This is very useful. Thank you very much.

MARION What on earth is it?

RONALD Well, it's – er – (*taking a stab at it*) – looks like a very nice set of pipe cleaners.

JANE Oh, no.

SIDNEY No, those aren't pipe cleaners.

RONALD Oh, aren't they?

SIDNEY Good gracious, no.

RONALD Oh, no. Silly of me. Just looked terribly like them for a minute. From a certain angle.

SIDNEY You should know those. It's a set of screwdrivers.

JANE Set of screwdrivers.

SIDNEY Electrical screwdrivers.

JANE You should know those, shouldn't you?

Sidney and Jane laugh. Marion opens her present

MARION (*with a joyous cry*) Oh, look! It's a lovely bottle of gin. Isn't that kind?

RONALD Oh, my God.

SIDNEY   Bit of Christmas spirit.

MARION   Lovely. I'll think of you when I'm drinking it.

JANE   (*still rummaging*) To the boys with love from Sidney and Jane. (*She produces two rather ghastly woolly toys – obviously unsuitable*)

SIDNEY   That's just a little something.

JANE   Just for their stockings in the morning.

MARION   Oh, how nice.

RONALD   They'll love these . . .

SIDNEY   That the lot?

JANE   No, I'm just trying to find the hm-mm.

SIDNEY   Well, it'll be at the bottom somewhere, I should think.

JANE   I've got it. It's nothing very much. We just got it this evening out of a cracker actually. We were going to keep it for our budgie but we thought your George might like it. For his collar. (*She holds up a little bell on a ribbon*)

EVA   Oh.

SIDNEY   So you'll know where he is.

JANE   As if you couldn't guess.

Sidney barks genially and hands them the bell

SIDNEY   Woof woof!

EVA   Thank you.

SIDNEY   (*to Geoffrey*) Woof woof. (*No response*) Woof woof.

GEOFFREY   (*flatly*) Thanks a lot.

SIDNEY   That's your lot. No more.

RONALD   I'm terribly sorry. I'm afraid we haven't got you anything at all. Not really much of ones for present buying.

SIDNEY   Oh, we didn't expect it.

JANE   No, no.

A pause. Sidney puts on a nose mask. Jane laughs. The others look horrified. Marion pours herself a gin

SIDNEY   Well – (*he pauses*) – you know who ought to be here now?

JANE Who?

SIDNEY Dick Potter. He'd start it off.

JANE With a bit of help from Lottie.

SIDNEY True. True.

RONALD Yes, well, for some odd reason we're all feeling a bit low this evening. Don't know why. But we were just all saying how we felt a bit down.

JANE Oh . . .

SIDNEY Oh dear oh dear.

RONALD Just one of those evenings, you know. The point is you'll have to excuse us if we're not our usual cheery selves.

MARION I'm perfectly cheery. I don't know about anybody else.

RONALD That is apart from my wife who is perfectly cheery.

SIDNEY Oh, that's quite understood.

JANE I have those sometimes, don't I?

SIDNEY You certainly do. You can say that again. Well, that's a shame.

RONALD Yes.

EVA (*after a slight pause*) My husband was saying to me just now, Sidney, that he feels terribly guilty that you keep on asking him to do jobs for you and he just hasn't been able to manage them.

SIDNEY Yes. Well, he's a busy man.

EVA Sometimes. But he really is dying to do something for you before long.

GEOFFREY Eh?

EVA He's really longing to.

SIDNEY Oh, well in that case, we'll see.

EVA If you could keep him in mind.

SIDNEY Yes, I'll certainly keep him in mind. Really rather depends.

GEOFFREY Yes, it does rather.

EVA He'd love to.

SIDNEY (*after a pause*) Well now, what shall we do? Anyone

87

got any ideas? We can't all sit round like this, can we? Not on Christmas Eve.

JANE No, not on Christmas Eve.

SIDNEY Spot of carpentry, spot of plumbing, eh? I know, what about a spot of electrical work? (*At the radio*) Well, we can have a bit of music to start off with, anyway. (*To Ronald*) This work all right, does it?

RONALD Yes, yes, but I wouldn't . . .

SIDNEY Get the party going, bit of music . . . (*He switches on the radio and begins to dance a little*)

JANE Bit of music'll get it going.

SIDNEY Hey . . .

JANE What?

SIDNEY You know what we ought to do now?

JANE What?

SIDNEY We ought to move all the chairs back and clear the floor and . . .

The radio warms up and the room is filled with the sound of an interminable Scottish reel which plays continually. Like most Scottish reels, without a break. This effectively drowns the rest of Sidney and Jane's discussion. He continues to describe with graphic gestures his idea to Jane. Jane claps her hands with excitement. They move the table, stove and chairs out of the way. Sidney then wheels the trolley away past Marion's armchair. She grabs a bottle as it goes by

RONALD (*yelling above the noise*) What the hell's going on?

SIDNEY (*yelling back*) You'll see. Just a minute. (*He turns the radio down a little*) Now then. We can't have this. We can't have all these glum faces, not at Christmas time.

JANE (*scurrying about collecting a bowl of fruit, a spoon, a tea-cosy, colander and tea towel from the dresser and draining-board*) Not at Christmas time. (*She opens the gin bottle and puts a glass near it on the trolley*)

SIDNEY So we're going to get you all jumping about. Get you cheerful.

RONALD No, well I don't think we really . . .

SIDNEY   No arguments, please.

RONALD   Yes, but all the same . . .

SIDNEY   Come on then, Eva, up you get.

EVA   (*uncertainly*) Well . . .

SIDNEY   Come on. Don't you let me down.

EVA   No . . . (*She rises*)

GEOFFREY   I'm afraid we both have to . . .

EVA   No, we don't. We'll play.

GEOFFREY   What do you mean, we'll . . .

EVA   If he wants to play, we'll play, darling.

Jane begins to roll up the carpet

SIDNEY   That's grand. That's marvellous. That's two – come on – any more?

MARION   What are we all doing? Is she going to be terribly sweet and wash our floor?

JANE   No, we're playing a game.

SIDNEY   A game.

MARION   Oh, what fun . . .

RONALD   Marion, I really don't think we should . . .

MARION   Oh, don't be such a misery, Ronnie. Come on.

RONALD   Oh . . .

SIDNEY   That's telling him, that's telling him. Now then listen very carefully, everyone. This is a version of musical chairs called Musical Dancing.

JANE   Musical Forfeits.

SIDNEY   Musical Dancing. It's called Musical Dancing.

JANE   Oh, I thought it was called Musical Forfeits.

SIDNEY   Musical Dancing. It's very simple. All you do – you start dancing round the room and when I stop the music you all have to freeze in the position you were last in . . .

Geoffrey sits on the high stool

Don't let him sit down. (*To Geoffrey*) Come on, get up.

EVA   (*sharply*) Get up.

Geoffrey gets up

SIDNEY   Only to make it more difficult, the last person caught
moving each time gets a forfeit. At the end, the person with
the least forfeits gets the prize. (*To Jane*) What's the prize
going to be?

JANE   (*producing it from the carrier*) A chocolate Father
Christmas.

SIDNEY   A chocolate Father Christmas, right. Everything
ready your end?

JANE   I think so.

SIDNEY   Got the list?

JANE   (*waving a scrap of paper*) Yes.

SIDNEY   Right. You take charge of the forfeits. I'll do the
music. Ready, everybody? Right. Off we go.

*Sidney turns up the music loud. The four stand looking faintly uneasy.
Jane and Sidney dance about to demonstrate*

Well, come on then. Come on. I don't call that dancing.
Everybody dance. Come on, dance about. Keep dancing till
the music stops.

*Marion starts to dance, in what she imagines to be a classical ballet
style. She is extremely shaky*

That's it. She's doing it. That's it. Look at her. Everybody
do what she's doing. Lovely.

The others begin sheepishly and reluctantly to hop about

And – stop! (*He cuts off the music*) Right. Who was the last?

JANE   Ron.

SIDNEY   Right. It's Ron. Ron has a forfeit. What's the first
one?

JANE   (*consulting her list*) Apple under the chin.

SIDNEY   Apple under his chin, right. Put an apple under his
chin.

RONALD   Eh? What are you doing?

Jane puts the apple under his chin

JANE   Here. Hold it. Go on, hold it.

RONALD   Oh, don't be so ridiculous, I can't possibly . . .

MARION   Oh, for heaven's sake, darling, do join in. We're all waiting for you. Don't be tedious.

RONALD   (*talking with difficulty*) This is absolutely absurd, I mean how am I to be . . .

SIDNEY   (*over this*) And off we go again. (*He turns up the music*)

They resume dancing. Marion is the only one who moves around: the others jig about on one spot. Sidney shouts encouragement

   And – stop! (*He stops the music*)

JANE   Eva!

SIDNEY   Right, Eva. What's Eva got?

JANE   (*consulting list*) Orange between the knees.

SIDNEY   Orange between the knees, right. If you drop it you get another forfeit automatically.

Jane gives Eva her orange

   And off we go again.

Music. From now on the forfeits come quick and fast. Jane reading them out, Sidney repeating them. Ronald gets the next (spoon in mouth). The music continues. Geoffrey gets the next (tea-cosy on head). They dance on. Marion gets the next (ironically, swallowing a gin in one). Ronald opens his mouth to protest at this last forfeit of Marion's. In doing so he drops his spoon

   (*Gleefully*) Another one for Ron!

JANE   Another one for Ron . . .

RONALD   What?

JANE   Pear on spoon in mouth . . .

SIDNEY   Pear on spoon in mouth . . . (*He gets up on the table and conducts*)

RONALD   Now listen I . . .

Jane rams the spoon handle back in Ronald's mouth. She balances a pear on the other end

SIDNEY And off we go . . .!

The permutations to this game are endless and Sidney's list covers them all. Under his increasingly strident commands, the dancers whirl faster and faster whilst accumulating bizarre appendages. Jane, the acolyte, darts in and out of the dancers with a dedicated frenzy. Geoffrey throws his tea-cosy to the floor. Jane picks it up and wraps a tea towel round his leg. She then pours another gin for Marion. Sidney, at the finish, has abandoned the idea of stopping the music. He screams at the dancers in mounting exhortation bordering on the hysterical

` That's it. Dance. Come on. Dance. Dance. Come on. Dance. Dance. Dance. Keep dancing. Dance . . .

It is on this scene that –

the CURTAIN *falls*

Glossary : reading the text

Act 1

1 *suburban*   lying on the outskirts of a town.

formica   hard plastic used for kitchen surfaces because it is easily cleaned.

dapper   neat.

unflappable   calm.

Yale knob   Yale locks open from the outside with a key; to open the door from the inside you simply turn the knob.

2 *Cats and dogs*   expression meaning heavy rain: it's raining cats and dogs.

fourth wall   imagine how the set would look on stage. In most theatres the audience would sit facing the three walls of the kitchen. We would look 'through' the imaginary fourth wall. So when Sidney looks at the clock on the fourth wall, he is actually looking into the audience.

eighteen-twenty-three   the Hopcroft house runs by the 24-hour clock: it is 6.23 pm.

3 *sailor's horn-pipe*   traditional sailors' dance.

5 *flies*   weak joke with a double meaning: flies can mean insects and the front of a man's trousers.

6 *pinny*   apron.

8 *ungraciously*   without kindness.

9 *mantelpiece*   shelf above a fireplace.

10 *soda siphons*   sealed bottles used to squirt soda water into drinks.

11 *dishy*   attractive – usually used to describe people.

13 *apartheid*   Marion misunderstands the label on the washing machine. It has separate programmes for white clothes and coloured clothes. Apartheid refers to the political system in which white and non-white people are treated separately. Ayckbourn cut this joke from his 1990 production.

icon   Marion misreads the label this time: an icon is a symbol.

poignant   sharp.

15 *knotty pine units*   manufactured wooden panels in which the knots in the wood are visible.

insistent   Marion's polite way of saying that she finds the colour of the curtains loud.

16 *drowned*   there is so much tonic water that the gin can hardly be tasted.

rheumatism   aching joints or muscles – a result of the spilt soda water.

17 *fraught*   tense.

18 *dismay*   alarm.

tentative   uncertain.

wellington boots   waterproof boots made of rubber.

plimsolls   light canvas shoes used for sport.

19 *trilby*   soft felt hat.

makes no ... appearance   Eva is not concerned about the impression she makes.

abstractly   without concentrating.

20 *gawps*   stares in amazement.

21 *yak*   type of ox with long shaggy hair.

22 *mistletoe*   evergreen shrub traditionally hung in houses at Christmas and underneath which people kiss.

23 *incredulous*   astonished.

24 *off-licence*   shop at which people can buy alcoholic drinks to consume at home.

25 *making the grade*   achieving success.

off the cuff   informal.

27 *striking while the iron is hot*   choosing the right moment to act.

goes off the boil   before the right moment is lost.

it's dog eat dog   it's a cruel world.

you scratch mine. I'll scratch yours...   you do me a favour and I'll do you a favour.

27 *Tit for tat*   you help me and I'll help you.

when the chips are down   at a time of crisis.

sanctuary   place of safety.

harem   group of women living with, or under the protection of, one man.

facets   sides (to his character).

well turned out   smart.

28 *Brownies*   junior members of the Guides, an organisation set up to develop girls' character and responsibility.

tickle   amuse.

29 *headway*   progress.

30 *cracker*   (slang) attractive woman.

P. and O.   passenger-ferry company.

31 *blazing*   hooting noisily.

still wide open   yet to be decided.

gleam in his eye   attractive idea that has not yet been developed.

32 *tentative*   cautious.

---

1   What are your first impressions of Jane and Sidney, and how do these change during the act?

2   From their behaviour, what can you tell about their differing attitudes to the party as the time for it to begin draws nearer (pages 1-9)?

3   How do Sidney and Ronald differ in their reactions to Geoffrey's suggestive remarks (pages 28-9)?

4   With the arrival of Geoffrey on page 27 all of the characters in the play have been introduced. Who do you find most sympathetic? Who do you find unsympathetic?

5   What do we learn of Jane's and Sidney's characters from their different actions once the party is over?

6   How does their marriage compare with the two others we have seen in Act 1?

Act 2

36 *bridge*   control room.

trendy homespun   simple but fashionable.

unkempt   untidy.

38 *nipped in for a quick one*   stopped at a pub for a brief drink.

sexual Flying Dutchman   legend has it that the Flying Dutchman sails the world without ever finding a port to stop in. Geoffrey sees his relationships with women in the same way.

39 *perpetrate*   be responsible for.

squalid   dirty and repulsive.

What I lack ... ethics   Geoffrey accepts that his sexual morality is unsound, but holds on to his high professional standards at work – which, he implies, Sidney Hopcroft does not possess.

40 *take a swing at*   try to hit.

by way of reprisal   to get back at me.

41 *vertigo*   feeling of giddiness caused by heights.

inert   limp.

42 *overwrought*   full of nervous tension.

43 *hubbub*   background noise of voices.

furtively   in a sly manner.

peaky   sickly.

44 *Mr Vim*   Vim is a well-known brand of kitchen cleaner.

couldn't see it for looking   it was so obvious that I didn't notice it.

45 *Muslims*   people who follow the religion of Islam. Geoffrey is suggesting that the neighbours will not need forks because they eat with their fingers.

Where there's a will   well-known saying: Where there's a will, there's a way, meaning if you are determined enough, you will find a solution to any problem.

elbow grease   vigorous rubbing.

46 *natter*   chat or gossip.

under the weather   unwell.

47 *Brace of shakes*   very quickly, as in two shakes of a lamb's tail.

prominent   obvious.

48 *crude noose*   rough loop tied in the washing line.

Where was Moses…?   a saying: Where was Moses when the lights went out?

on the go   busy.

flex   plastic-covered electric cable.

49 *except the kitchen sink*   another of Sidney's feeble jokes. Everything except the kitchen sink suggests he has brought every possible tool up with him.

50 *thingummyjig*   all-purpose word people use when they cannot think of the exact word they want.

short   short-circuit: the unprotected wires could connect.

51 *grubs*   small headless screws.

52 *Each to his own*   each person is to concentrate on his or her own task.

pins   (slang) legs. Marion's drinking has made her unsteady.

53 *lucky hunches*   feelings or ideas that have proved to be successful.

paint stripper   powerful chemical used to remove old paint.

54 *Scouts*   organisation for boys to encourage character building and responsibility.

jumble   second-hand items for a jumble sale which are sold in order to raise money for a particular charity or organisation.

55 *Rabies*   potentially fatal disease carried in the saliva of some animals and associated particularly with mad dogs.

groggy   dazed.

56 *patent medicines*   medicines available without a doctor's prescription.

vital   lively.

58 *obscene*   disgusting.

whatjamacallit … thingy … whosit   all purpose words used when you cannot recall the exact word you want. See note to page 50.

59 *recoils* pulls back.

60 *bits and bobs* various items.

61 *you-know-whats* underwear.

  ludicrous ridiculous.

62 *Upsidaisy* word used when helping up a child.

63 *singlet* vest.

64 *liability* hazard.

  oblivious unaware of everything around her.

  abjectly hopelessly.

65 *bedraggled quintet* untidy group of five.

  unabated as loudly as ever.

---

1 Ignoring the mess, what does the Jacksons' kitchen tell you about them?

2 How do you respond to Geoffrey after his lengthy monologue (pages 37-40)? Does it increase or reduce your sympathy for him?

3 On page 53 Ronald refers to Sidney's financial success over the past year. What signs are there that the fortunes of the other characters have moved up or down?

4 What do we learn about all the characters on stage from the fact that in attempting to help Eva they simply embark on separate DIY tasks?

5 How many of the events that took place in this act were you able to predict – the water down the sink? Ronald's electric shock? George biting Dick Potter? Does it make the play more or less funny that you can see certain jokes coming?

6 Before turning to Act 3, predict what you think is going to happen. Will there be a party? How will the different marriages have changed? What will be the conclusion of the play?

Act 3

66 *Aga range* large stove fuelled by coal, wood or oil.

eye-shade plastic visor worn on the forehead to shield the eyes from overhead light.

on the blink out of order.

67 *Whitsun* Christian holiday held seven weeks after Easter.

68 *craving* desire. Ronald worries about Marion's cravings because of the tradition that pregnant women crave unusual food.

bootees knitted boots for babies.

sedative drug to calm people down.

stimulant drug to make people more active.

69 *mutual* shared.

71 *Trans-Siberian Express* Ronald compares the drinks trolley to the train that travels across arctic Russia.

depleted low.

knocking them off stealing them.

73 *flair* talent.

unprepossessing unimpressive.

74 *bedroom bell* reminder of the past when each room in large middle-class houses had a bell to summon the servants.

75 *knocked off* finished.

taken off fled.

call it a day finish (the marriage).

Under the bridge well-known saying: That's all water under the bridge, meaning those events are all in the past and cannot be returned to.

seem to have the hang of it seem to have the talent to cope.

closed book mystery.

come apart at the seams Ronald sees both of his marriages following the same pattern: both have fallen to pieces after some time.

77 *negligée*   woman's lightweight dressing gown.

Scrooge   Charles Dickens' character Scrooge is well known as a miser.

78 *old sausage*   silly, but touching, term of affection.

unutterably   unspeakably.

81 *goodies*   various treats.

trifle   dessert of sponge, fruit, custard, cream, and usually sherry.

82 *lamely*   feebly.

83 *blower*   party toy which, when blown, unwraps into a tube and makes a squeaking noise.

84 *'nuff*   enough.

hm-mm   Jane indicates the object without wanting to mention it by name, which would spoil the surprise.

85 *taking a stab at it*   guessing.

86 *cracker*   traditional Christmas novelty. Two people pull it from each end and it cracks open, revealing a toy, a paper hat and a printed joke.

budgie   budgerigar – a small, colourful caged bird.

87 *low*   depressed.

88 *interminable*   endless.

Scottish reel   music for a lively dance.

glum   sad.

89 *musical chairs*   game in which everyone circles around chairs until the music stops suddenly and the players have to find a seat. There is always one chair less than the number of players.

90 *forfeit*   penalty, usually something embarrassing to do.

91 *tea-cosy*   fabric cover placed over a tea-pot to keep the tea hot.

92 *strident*   loud and harsh.

accumulating bizarre appendages   receiving strange objects.

acolyte   assistant.

exhortation   strong persuasion.

1 Are you surprised at the change that has overcome Eva (pages 66-9)? How do you explain it?

2 How is Ronald different when compared to what you remember of him in the previous two acts?

3 Why do you think the couples are so eager not to see the Hopcrofts?

4 How do you think Jane and Sidney have changed since the last party?

5 Why doesn't Ronald simply refuse to join in the game?

6 How would you describe Sidney's character as he keeps the game going at the end of the act?

7 What does the game show about the way the relationships between all the characters have changed since Act 1?

▓ Study programme

Performance projects

1️⃣ Compile a theatre programme based on *Absurd Person Singular*. It should include the following:

- cover;
- cast list [you decide on the actors];
- brief outline of the play;
- brief background on Alan Ayckbourn;
- discussion of two key themes;
- review of a theatre/television production of the play – including actors' performances, costumes, setting, lighting;
- your personal response to the play.

Spend some time planning the *design* in rough. Look through magazines and theatre programmes to collect ideas for headings, use of photographs, visually exciting layout of pages.

Then look through programmes to see the kind of writing style they use: are they aimed at the general or specialist reader? Do they contain any jargon words? Do they offer an objective view of the play and the performance or do they serve simply as publicity?

Write your text out first in rough, so that you can then check it through to improve accuracy of punctuation and spelling. Use a reference book to show you the wide variety of stage spaces which are available to the directors. For the background on Alan Ayckbourn, see 'Suggestions for further reading', page 117.

2️⃣ In groups, record a radio production of one act of the play. Before you begin, think about which act might best lend itself to translation onto radio. Use these points to guide you through the recording process:

- decide which act to perform;
- assign parts;
- consider problems raised by the medium of radio – for example, the fly spray jokes in Act 1;
- decide upon necessary sound effects, theme music, and how to convey the visual clues contained in the stage directions – how, for example, will you convey to listeners the décor of the various kitchens?
- rehearse in a group; then, if possible, practise your own part at home; then rehearse using the tape recorder. Listen back and discuss the result;
- record the finished performance;
- play a brief extract of your production to the rest of the class;
- dub the various groups' different productions on to one tape ready for classes studying the play next year.

Write about the problems you encountered in recording the extract for radio. How did you overcome them? What are the advantages and disadvantages of presenting *Absurd Person Singular* on radio?

3 Take home a recording made by one of the other groups. Write a review of their production. First read a radio review from a newspaper to help you to find the appropriate style. You might comment upon:

- overall clarity;
- characterisation (do the characters come to life? Do they sound as you imagine them?);
- acting performances which came across particularly successfully;
- fluency and pace of the production;
- use of music and sound effects.

4 As well as being a writer, Alan Ayckbourn is also a full-time director at the Stephen Joseph Theatre-in-the-Round in Scarborough. Here is what he says about the business of directing a play:

I remember what Stephen Joseph once said to me. It was when I was wrestling with that first play, Gaslight, and I asked him what directing was about and he replied, 'You have to create an atmosphere in which the actors themselves can create.' I said, 'Thank you very much,' but, of course, it's the most difficult thing to achieve. I've been trying to do so ever since.

Judith Cook, *Directors' Theatre*

For this activity you will need to work out quite carefully in advance who you want to work with in a small group. Together you need to choose a brief extract from *Absurd Person Singular* (say three pages). Try to choose a scene which has the same number of characters as the number of people in your group *minus one*. This person is going to direct your performance.

Once you have chosen your scene, assign the parts. The director needs now to start working on that special 'atmosphere' Alan Ayckbourn refers to above, deciding or discussing (depending on your approach!) which kind of stage you will use, whether to use furniture that is to hand as part of the scenery and so on.

Next, sitting down, you should read through the scene, and at this point the director might want simply to listen or to make notes. You might feel that there are some points related to each actor's reading which are worth clarifying early on – speaking too quickly, in too flat a voice, with too corny an accent. Remember, though, that people rarely read well without preparation.

Alan Ayckbourn's approach to directing is to get actors moving about, acting out the play with their texts in front of them, early on. Other directors like to spend much more time discussing the ideas of the play. When you are ready you should begin to act out the play, the director keeping notes and giving advice at the end. Obviously you are going to need to rehearse over and over again regardless of whether you are going to hold on to the scripts for the final performance.

Gradually as you rehearse, a rhythm of performance will build up, the extract will become natural and funny; actors will try out new ways of speaking and moving; the director will give feedback. Work on preparing a polished performance to show to the rest of the class. Most importantly, though, don't *under*-rehearse. Even though rehearsing the same brief extract over and over will become monotonous, it will add to your confidence in performance.

5 Once you have performed your brief extract, write about the role you played in the group:

- Did you contribute ideas and make suggestions, or were you more hesitant or even negative?

- What did you learn about your character? What different ways of playing him or her did you try out?

- How did you find the experience of directing? Did it feel natural, daunting, difficult? Explain. How did the actors respond to your suggestions?

- Describe the rehearsal process: how many times did you run through the scene? How much time did you spend initially on discussing the extract? Did you stop after each run-through to discuss your work? How, with hindsight, could the rehearsal process have been made more effective?

- How successful was the final performance? How did it compare with your best rehearsal? How did the audience respond?

- Finally, describe any new insights you have gained into *Absurd Person Singular* from this intensive work on the play.

6 Work in small groups of, say, four people. Think of a 'style' in which you would like to see an extract from *Absurd Person Singular* performed. Some possible styles might be:

- pantomime;
- silent movie;
- melodrama;
- opera;
- Agatha Christie whodunnit;
- children's television;
- western.

Now challenge another group to perform one page of the play (you choose which one) in the style you specify.

7 Imagine you were asked to direct *Absurd Person Singular* for the theatre. Write about the type of stage you would use (find a reference book so that you are aware of the possibilities), explaining why you think it would be most suitable. Then choose one character and imagine you were addressing the actor who is to play him or her. Write about the character, discussing his or her background, mannerisms, way of speaking, importance in the play, and so on.

8 Design a poster to advertise your own production of the play. What would be the central image of the poster? What quotation or slogan would you use to accompany the picture? Which well-known actors and actresses would you cast to play the various roles?

9 Write a review of the television version of *Absurd Person Singular* (BBC-TV 1985). What are the problems of using well-known actors and actresses to play the parts? Were any of the characters different from the way you had imagined them? What are the advantages and disadvantages of presenting the play on television rather than on the stage?

10 Write the beginning of your own Act 4 of *Absurd Person Singular*. Where will it take place – Dick and Lottie Potters' kitchen? How have the characters changed over the year? Remember to include the various running jokes and distinctive speech styles of the characters.

11 Imagine that the television production of the play is about to be repeated. Write a 'blurb' about *Absurd Person Singular* for the *Radio Times*. Think who the audience will be: what will they need to know in advance in order to attract them to watch the programme? Look at the *Radio Times*. How many words are used for such blurbs? Limit yourself to this number.

Characters

☐ Draw a graph to show how the characters change emotionally during the play. Along the horizontal axis show the passage of time, from the beginning of Act 1 to the end of Act 3. Along the vertical axis devise a scale which indicates the full range of emotional high and low points. Plot each character's fortune in a different colour, putting in brackets the event which forms a peak or trough. Compare your finished graph with others in the class. Use your graph to answer these questions:

- Which character, according to your graph, reaches the highest emotional level?
- Which character reaches the lowest?
- Which character has the greatest range in his or her emotions throughout the play?
- Which character has the narrowest range?

How useful is the graph in displaying the characters' emotional developments throughout the play? How could it be made more sensitive or more informative?

☐ It is Act 1. Dick and Lottie have been abandoned in the sitting-room (for example, pages 11-14). With a partner, improvise their conversation. Are they just as hearty alone together as they are in company? Do they find it suspicious that they should have been deserted by the other couples in this way?

☐ Originally, Alan Ayckbourn wrote *Absurd Person Singular* with the events set in the sitting-room. Rewrite the play from page 17 (*silence*) to page 19 (*Eva comes in*): Jane and Sidney are frantically searching for the tonic water in the kitchen. But what is being said in the sitting-room between Ronald and Marion, and Dick and Lottie?

To do this well, you will need to try to capture each character's way of speaking. Don't be afraid to include pauses. Remember that the Potters might well dominate the conversation, giving you a chance to show how the other characters react to them. The couples might quite quickly realise they have little in common and fall silent – or perhaps the Potters would never realise this and would never fall silent!

Once you have written your script, read it through in a small group, and then discuss how successful you feel your characterisation has been.

4 In 'The writer on writing' on page vii, Alan Ayckbourn says:

Nowhere in the house says more about a person's habit and background, the nature of their day-to-day existence, than their kitchen.

Imagine a television programme that takes you through the keyhole into the homes of famous people. Imagine you went into one of the three kitchens seen in the play. What could you tell about the people who lived in that house? Improvise a two-minute sketch based on this idea.

Alternatively, imagine we have moved some years further on in time. Sidney is a successful businessman. Jane is showing television viewers around her new kitchen and comparing it with the one we see in the play. What do you think would be the features of the Hopcrofts' new kitchen?

5 Put together a television chat show in which Jane and Sidney (now a highly successful businessman) discuss their rising fortunes. What are their memories of the parties of Acts 1 and 2?

Or how about *This is Your Life?* Sidney is the surprise victim, and other guests are brought on stage, one by one, to share their memories. Just before dirty water was poured over him, Sidney predicted: *We'll be laughing about this* (Act 2, page 62). Are the characters' memories of the parties happy?

6 Alan Ayckbourn has said, *All my characters have flaws and are pock-marked.* Draw up a table which includes all the characters and lists their various flaws, from most trivial to most serious. Looking at this, decide which character in the play appears the most flawed. Compare your table with a friend's and see if you agree.

7 In *Absurd Person Singular* some of the characters can be identified

not only from *what* they say, but also from their *style* of speech. Look at the characters in turn and draw up a list of what is distinctive about their way of speaking.

8 Sidney talks frequently in clichés – well-worn phrases. Make a list of ten of these from the play. What do they tell you about his character? Over the next few days, keep a notebook handy and write down clichés you hear in conversation, on television, or that you read in newspapers. In which situation did you come across the most? Why do you think people use clichés?

9 Look again at Ronald's long speech in Act 3, page 75, in which he talks about the way his marriage has disintegrated like an old jacket. Write a similar speech for Marion. What were her ideals and how have they been lost?

10 Look again at Sidney and Jane's arrival at the icy kitchen in Act 3. Make a list of the ways in which these two characters have changed since we first saw them.

11 Choose one sentence from the play which you think represents each character. Find a photograph in a magazine which most resembles your image of the character. Paste these together – the picture and the quotation – and compare your collage with those which others in the class have made.

12 Geoffrey's ambitious shopping centre has just collapsed. The media splash the story across the nation's front pages and television screens. Write or improvise an interview in which he talks about what went wrong. Look back to Act 2, page 37, for precise details of the scheme.

13 Write an extract from the diary of Sidney and another from the diary of Marion after the first Christmas party. How does Sidney think the party went? How does this compare with Marion's perceptions of the evening? If you prefer, choose two other contrasting characters and write their diaries.

14 Write a letter from Geoffrey to Sidney (or even from Eva on Geoffrey's behalf) asking to be considered for a job. Write Sidney's reply, bearing in mind the clichés he uses when he speaks: try to incorporate these into his letter of reply.

15 Discuss the character you feel greatest sympathy for. Explain why, and then compare your choice with someone else's.

16 Improvise the scene early in Act 2 in which Jane and Sidney have arrived at Geoffrey and Eva's party and are left alone in the sitting-room (pages 41-2). Bearing in mind what you know about the characters, present the conversation which might take place.

17 Ronald and Marion, Geoffrey and Eva are all characters whose lives have turned sour in middle age. Take them back in time to their youth. What would they have been like as teenagers, or in their early twenties? Discuss or improvise your ideas.

18 Which two characters in the play are most dissimilar? Improvise a conversation between them in the sitting-room. What would they have to talk about?

19 Read the following statements about *Absurd Person Singular*. For each one decide whether you think the statement is true (T), not true (NT), or that there is not enough evidence to decide (NEE). You will, of course, need to look back at the text in order to check some of your answers and you will need to be able to support your point of view with evidence from the play when you discuss your opinions.

Act 1

1 Sidney Hopcroft is a successful businessman.

2 Jane enjoys parties.

3 Marion is very outspoken.

4 Ronald is interested in the Hopcrofts' kitchen.

5 Eva is already contemplating suicide.

6   Geoff is admired by the two other men.

7   Sidney's way of speaking shows that he belongs to a different class from the other characters.

8   Jane and Sidney are happily married.

9   Alan Ayckbourn finds Dick and Lottie irritating.

10 No one notices that Jane spends most of the party in the rain.

Act 2

11 The Jacksons' kitchen is fashionable.

12 It was Eva's decision that she and Geoff should separate.

13 Geoff accepts responsibility for his affairs with other women.

14 Jane cleans the oven as a favour to Eva.

15 Marion's drinking has become more serious compared to last Christmas.

16 It was obvious from the start of the act that Jane would pour the bowl of water down the sink.

17 Marion's attitude to her husband's shock is cruel (page 61).

18 Sidney's remarks to Jane, after she pours greasy water over him, are cruel (page 63).

19 Only one character realises that Eva has been trying to kill herself.

20 All the characters have changed a little since Act 1.

Act 3

21 Eva's change of personality is unexpected.

22 Marion is staying in her room following a disagreement with Ronald.

23 Ronald is secretly worried about Marion's drink problem.

24 Eva and Geoffrey's marriage is happy.

25 Geoffrey and Ronald are both dependent on Sidney Hopcroft's favour.

26 Jane is more confident in this act.

27 Sidney has come around to show how successful he has become.

28 There is something unpleasant about Sidney's games.

29 Act 3 is less funny than Act 2 but funnier than Act 1.

30 The characters could refuse to dance if they wanted to.

Bear in mind as you discuss your answers that some of the questions cannot simply be answered as true or false: different people will respond differently. It is therefore important that you are able to *explain* your response precisely.

20 Imagine Sidney Hopcroft some years on. He is now well known as a self-made millionaire and has published his autobiography. Write an extract in which he thinks back over the events of the three years covered in the play.

21 Have a game of *What the Ayckbourn?*, a quiz based on **Absurd Person Singular**. Here are some possible rounds with examples to show the kinds of questions involved (correct answers below):

1 **Identify the quotation**
   Who says, *Don't tell me it does the ironing too?*

2 **Odd line out**
   Which of these quotations is NOT spoken by Sidney?

   (a) *A small spillage. My fault.*
   (b) *I've partitioned off the spare bedroom as a walk-in cupboard for the wife.*
   (c) *I'm sorry about that, Jane. I really am.*
   (d) *Everything except the kitchen sink, and that's already here, eh?*

3 **Fill in the missing word**

   RONALD: *I meant the Harrison thing. Hear it ***** ***** ...Oh, I'm sorry, perhaps that's the wrong expression to use – bit unfortunate.*

Work in small teams to devise three questions for each round. Try to think up questions that become increasingly difficult, but which are not impossible. You might, of course, be able to think of different types of rounds.

Round one is an 'open' round. First hand up with the correct answer wins two points. If an answer is incorrect it can be passed to another team for one point if they answer correctly.

Further rounds are played by asking questions directly to one team at a time. The points system remains the same.

Answer to sample quiz questions: 1 Marion; 2(c); 3 *fell through*.

Themes

1️⃣ Look at the list of themes below. Put them in order of those you consider most important in the play to those that are least important. You might feel that some are irrelevant to *Absurd Person Singular* in which case you can leave these out. Equally, you might think of a theme which is not already included in the list: add it to yours. Then compare your list with someone else's and explain your choices.

1 marriage	9 cruelty
2 problems involved in keeping pets	10 language
3 money	11 theatre
4 social class	12 growing older
5 Christmas	13 telling lies
6 alcoholism	14 loneliness
7 success	15 selfishness
8 parties	

2️⃣ Discuss the effect of switching around Acts 2 and 3 as some American producers wanted to do. How would the play have been different? What would have been the positive and negative effects on the play as a whole?

3️⃣ Choose either Act 1 or Act 2 and show what happens in the plot by drawing a diagram of the main events. Move from the left of the page to the right and watch how events become increasingly more complicated and tangled up. Compare your finished diagram with a friend's.

4 Think of those dramatic movie trailers you see in the cinema. Imagine a film of *Absurd Person Singular* has been made. How would you advertise it? Produce a storyboard for a thirty-second trailer which highlights the main images you would use – which scenes? Which characters saying which lines? – and write the voice-over that would accompany the images. Then write a paragraph explaining what you tried to achieve in your trailer. What were your aims? What aspects of the play did you wish to emphasise – the comedy, the farce, the sadness?

5 *Absurd Person Singular* was written in the early seventies. Look through the text and see if there are any details which make the play feel dated. If you were directing the play today, would you update it into the nineties, or try to give it a flavour of the seventies?

Draw stage and costume designs for the production, using reference books for accuracy. Then write about your plans, explaining why you have chosen to present the play in this way.

6 The Introduction to this edition on page xiii suggests that *Absurd Person Singular* is partly concerned with the idea of class. How could you show this on stage in the costumes the characters wear? How would the various characters dress in Act 1? Which characters would be wearing clothes of a different style by Act 3? Describe these changes.

7 Discuss why the play is set at Christmas. Is this a limitation in some ways? Could the three acts in fact be set at parties occurring at any time of the year? What would the differences be?

8 Discuss the idea of success. What do we learn about success from the play? What is your definition of success? To be wealthy, or happy? To have a good job, or material possessions, or a family? Which character do you most resemble in your ambitions?

9 *Absurd Person Singular* presents a rather bleak picture of marriage. Discuss what has gone wrong in the various partnerships. Who is to blame? Do you detect any hope that some of the relationships between the couples will improve? How successful do you consider the marriage

between Sidney and Jane? What, do you think, was the attraction between them?

10. In groups, discuss the following questions:

- Which did you find the funniest moment in the play?
- Which was the saddest moment?
- Which was the most disturbing moment?
- What is the main theme of the play?
- Which character would you most like to play? Why?

11. What if …?

Discuss how the play would have been different if the following events had taken place:

- Sidney had gone out for the tonic water leaving Jane at the party;
- Marion had told the truth about her feelings for the Hopcrofts' home;
- Dick and Lottie had been more concerned to know what was happening in the kitchen;
- Eva had the drink problem and Marion was attempting suicide;
- Sidney's business had crashed between Act 2 and Act 3.

Do you consider any of these possibilities too far-fetched even to discuss? Explain why.

12. The introduction to this edition on page xiii says that *Absurd Person Singular* might seem a rather remote play to some readers at first sight. What information do you think a reader needs to be told in advance in order to gain the most pleasure from the play? Write a brief introduction that does this more successfully than the one provided.

13. Discuss parties. Why do people hold them? What is their purpose? What factors make a successful party and an unsuccessful one?

14. Think of a new title for *Absurd Person Singular*, one which you think is more appropriate. Write a paragraph to explain your choice.

Study questions

1. Choose one or more of the following topics to discuss and write about:

- Choose three characters and examine the way in which they change during the play.

- Discuss what the three different kitchens show us about each pair of characters.

- What does the play show us about the way people treat one another in public and in private?

- How far do you think the play is rooted in the early seventies?

- What do you learn of marriage from *Absurd Person Singular*?

- Describe each couple in turn. What do you think attracted them to one another in the first place and what are the problems you can detect now in their marriages?

- What are the signs, in his language and behaviour, that Sidney Hopcroft is socially beneath his guests?

- Which character do you think changes most during the play? Explain your answer.

- What evidence is there in *Absurd Person Singular* to support the idea that Alan Ayckbourn's skills as a playwright grow out of his background as a practical man of the theatre?

- Choose your favourite moment from the play and explain what it is that you like about it.

- How far would you agree that *Absurd Person Singular* is typically English?

- Think back to your first impressions of *Absurd Person Singular*. Describe the way in which these have changed as you have studied the play in greater detail.

- How far would you agree that men and women are shown to be radically different from one another in *Absurd Person Singular*?

- Choose two contrasting characters and describe how they differ in their perceptions of success.

- What are the different forms of laughter the play provokes? Pinpoint the different types of jokes Ayckbourn uses.

2 Discuss and write about the following statements:

- For all the comedy, the ending of *Absurd Person Singular* is deeply pessimistic.

- Not a single character comes out of *Absurd Person Singular* free from criticism.

- *Absurd Person Singular* illustrates a gulf that exists between men and women.

- The saddest character in *Absurd Person Singular* is Jane.

- *Absurd Person Singular* is actually three separate plays: a social comedy, a black farce, and a straight play.

- The running jokes in *Absurd Person Singular* make parts of the plot highly predictable. Ironically, this makes the play more, rather than less, amusing.

- *Absurd Person Singular* warns us about the association between power and money.

- The dumbshow in Act 2 of *Absurd Person Singular* is a miscalculation on Alan Ayckbourn's part: it reduces the credibility of the play as a whole.

Suggestions for further reading

Other plays by Alan Ayckbourn

Alan Ayckbourn has written more than thirty-five plays, not all of them published. If you wish to read some, the following list includes those which are most easily obtained:

The Norman Conquests

Three related plays, in which the same situation is seen from three different locations. The three plays are *Table Manners*, *Living Together* and *Round and Round the Garden*. The plays were all recorded for television by ITV in 1977.

Three Plays
One volume containing *Bedroom Farce, Absurd Person Singular* and *Absent Friends*. *Bedroom Farce* was recorded for television by ITV in 1980, the others by the BBC in 1985.

Joking Apart and Other Plays
Another collection, this time of four Ayckbourn plays: *Joking Apart, Just Between Ourselves, Ten Times Table* and *Sisterly Feelings*. *Just Between Ourselves* was recorded for television by ITV in 1978.

Woman in Mind
A woman creates an imaginary family because her own family is so boring. But the audience learns that Susan's imagination cannot be trusted.

Works by other playwrights

Ayckbourn has said that various playwrights influenced him. For comparison you might like to look in particular at the following:

Rhinoceros, The Chairs, The Lesson   by Eugene Ionesco
Three plays by an influential 'absurdist' writer. In *Rhinoceros*, for example, a group of people go about their business in the market place when a live rhinoceros charges through!

The Caretaker   by Harold Pinter
Pinter was possibly the strongest influence on Ayckbourn's style: the dialogue becomes increasingly odd, the everyday conversation disguising the menace beneath the surface.

Works about Alan Ayckbourn

Conversations with Ayckbourn   by Ian Watson
The single most useful critical text. Ayckbourn talks fascinatingly about his background in the theatre, his approach to writing, his work as a director. Easy, entertaining and informative reading.

File on Ayckbourn   by Malcolm Page

Wider reading assignments

1 Compare *Absurd Person Singular* with any other Alan Ayckbourn plays you have read. Would you agree with Ayckbourn that *Absurd Person Singular* is possibly *the nearest to a black farce that I've written*? Describe the different kinds of humour evident in the different plays.

2 From the Ayckbourn plays which you have read, what would you say were his main themes? What do you learn about these? Is there any evidence that his attitude to some of the themes has changed over the years?

3 Compare *Absurd Person Singular* with a play by either Ionesco or Pinter. Look particularly at the writing style. What are the similarities and differences? How far would you agree that *Absurd Person Singular* contains elements of absurdism in its plotting and dialogue? Which of the plays is the more entertaining and which has the more disturbing effect?

Longman Group UK Limited,
*Longman House, Burnt Mill, Harlow,
Essex CM20 2JE, England*
and Associated Companies throughout the world.

First published 1991

*Editorial material set in 10/12 point Helvetica Light Condensed
Produced by Longman Singapore Publishers (Pte) Ltd,
Printed in Singapore*

ISBN 0 582 06020 6

Acknowledgements

My thanks to the two enthusiastic classes who performed *Absurd Person
Singular* with me in lessons, generating so much laughter in the process.

Geoff Barton

Consultants: Linda Cookson
                   Geoff Barton

Cover illustration: background by Jonathan Bentley; inset by Kathy Baxendale.